D0747283

## Praise for *Ultimate Guide to Platform Building*

People will tell you that you are the brand. Wendy Keller just wrote the definitive guide on how to build you into your own brand worthy of followers.

—JEFFREY HAYZLETT, PRIMETIME TV AND PODCAST HOST, CHAIRMAN OF C-SUITE NETWORK, AUTHOR OF *THINK BIG, ACT BIGGER*

I have consulted with hundreds of entrepreneurs during my career. The most successful build a community of raving fans who love them and what they do. Wendy Keller's book is the best I have read on building a strong platform to grow your fan base. It covers all the relevant tools: social media, podcasts, videos, blogs, speeches, and workshops. It is a must read for aspiring entrepreneurs, business owners, and company executives. In this age of technology acceleration, I don't think it is possible to build a great business without strong platform-building skills. So read the book, implement the practices, and watch your business grow.

—MICHAEL GLAUSER, EXECUTIVE DIRECTOR OF THE CLARK CENTER FOR ENTREPRENEURSHIP AT UTAH STATE UNIVERSITY, AUTHOR OF *MAIN STREET ENTREPRENEUR*

Wendy Keller understands that you have to make every second count in marketing and that it's more important to serve than to sell.

—AMY PORTERFIELD, ONLINE MARKETING STRATEGIST

The positioning tips in Chapter 4 all by themselves are worth the price of admission. The *Ultimate Guide to Platform Building* is a step-by-step manual to building a tangible presence in a competitive marketplace that raises your fees and causes demand to rise. If you use this book as your "make sure we don't miss anything in our public presence" manual, you'll never make a major omission. She covers vital details like audio production and what colors to wear in a video shoot—something I've never seen in a book of this type. It's comprehensive.

—PERRY MARSHALL, AUTHOR OF *ULTIMATE GUIDE TO GOOGLE ADWORDS*, *ULTIMATE GUIDE TO FACEBOOK ADVERTISING*, *80/20 SALES AND MARKETING*, AND *EVOLUTION 2.0*

Wendy Keller's book on platform building is a practical, exceptionally comprehensive book on how to distinguish yourself or your business. The selection of ideas will help every reader to find tactics that are realistic and easy to implement. Whether you are a small business owner, a doctor, lawyer, life coach, therapist, author, retailer, musician, painter or even run an auto body shop, this book will help you grow your business and make more money.

—Ford Saeks, CEO of Prime Concepts Group, Marketing Strategist, Speaker

One of the trends I note heavily for businesses of all shapes and sizes in the future is how we are entering a new creative age driven by a D.I.Y. ethos unleashed due to platform technology. Wendy Keller uses a very personal approach to help you become a solopreneur or small-business owner who doesn't look at the world of entrepreneurship as an obstacle, but an advantage. Read this to learn and execute on how the platform economy will help you grow your business in perpetuity.

—Geoffrey Colon, Communications Designer at Microsoft, Author of *Disruptive Marketing*

Growing a platform is the most important step any entrepreneur can take to get leads flowing into their business. Wendy's book is a great primer on the basics and her suggestions for how to delegate it most effectively so it gets done right and on time are excellent. I've built several businesses in my career and the number one thing I know is you must delegate everything you can to save your energy and brain cells for big thinking.

—Daven Michaels, CEO of 123Employee, Author of *New York Times'* Bestseller *Outsource Smart*

Entrepreneur MAGAZINE'S

# ULTIMATE
# GUIDE TO
# Platform
# BUILDING

- Develop content that converts fans into customers
- Create a platform strategy that multiplies your marketing efforts **overnight**
- Showcase your brand, product, or company and attract new opportunities

Entrepreneur
**PRESS**®

WENDY KELLER

Entrepreneur Press, Publisher
Cover Design: Andrew Welyczko
Production and Composition: Eliot House Productions

© 2016 by Entrepreneur Media, Inc.
All rights reserved.
Reproduction or translation of any part of this work beyond that permitted by Section 107 or 108
of the 1976 United States Copyright Act without permission of the copyright owner is unlawful.
Requests for permission or further information should be addressed to the Business Products
Division, Entrepreneur Media Inc.

This publication is designed to provide accurate and authoritative information in regard to the
subject matter covered. It is sold with the understanding that the publisher is not engaged in
rendering legal, accounting or other professional services. If legal advice or other expert assistance is
required, the services of a competent professional person should be sought.

**Library of Congress Cataloging-in-Publication Data**
    Names: Keller, Wendy, 1964– author.
    Title: Entrepreneur Magazine's ultimate guide to platform building/Wendy Keller.
    Description: Irvine: Entrepreneur Press, 2016. | Series: Ultimate series
    Identifiers: LCCN 2016035900| ISBN 978-159918-598-9 (paperback) | ISBN 1-59918-598-9 |
        ISBN 978-161308-353-6 (e-ISBN)
    Subjects: LCSH: Branding (Marketing) | Advertising. | Small business. | Strategic planning. |
        BISAC: BUSINESS & ECONOMICS/Small Business. | BUSINESS & ECONOMICS/
        Development/Business Development. | BUSINESS & ECONOMICS / Leadership. |
        BUSINESS & ECONOMICS / Advertising & Promotion.
    Classification: LCC HF5415.1255 .K454 2016 | DDC 658.8/27—dc23
    LC record available at https://lccn.loc.gov/2016035900

Printed in the United States of America

21  20  19  18  17                                                                    10 9 8 7 6 5 4 3 2 1

# Contents

# How to Get the Most Benefit from This Book

Chances are, you are reading this book for a specific, measurable purpose: you want your platform to grow so that you make more money. These pages deliver on that, big time. One early reader, a highly successful and renowned marketing consultant, told me, "I actually took notes on your good ideas here. I plan to use one of these ideas with my clients."

I figure you've got three choices.

1. You can read a whole lot of good stuff in here, not do any of it, and get frustrated because nothing changes in your business. Owning a book doesn't mean you'll magically get the results it could deliver. In the publishing industry, we call the whole genre "shelf help" because unread books help no one but the shelf.

2. You could do some of this stuff haphazardly and give up when it doesn't work on the first try. We may as well start with the truth: Some things will work OK. Some things won't work for you at all (although they have worked for others). But for certain, some of the strategies in here could help you hit your ball out of the park! *Note*: You'll need to give it more than one measly shot, in most cases. A little tweaking and customizing may be required. That's just business.

3. You could decide to trust the process. The ideas and strategies you are about to receive are based on what has really worked for the hundreds of people whose businesses I've helped grow. "Don't knock it 'til you try it." Let's say you wanted to play the violin. You could watch some YouTube videos and get the basic idea. You could buy a violin and practice some chords. It would be true that now you know "how" to play the violin. Bravo! But until you practice, learn, adapt, and grow, would people pay to listen to you? Probably not.

My goal with this book is to turn you into a platform-building virtuoso. We're going to build a platform together that is customized to your goals, your business, your talents, interests, and abilities. But just like everything else, "practice makes perfect."

I recommend that you begin with Chapters 1 through 5, which cover the fundamentals. When you are clear on those, the rest will make a lot more sense. Those first chapters can easily be read in one sitting, and they lay down the foundation for the rest of the book. Also, in them you will get a bonus: a free assessment that will help you choose your personal best options from the large selection of ideas offered in these pages..

When you get to the good stuff—the strategies—at first just choose a few options that appeal to you. Test them out. Try them on. Adjust them to fit. See how much you like doing them, and if you like the results you are getting. Give yourself three to six months to try them out. A strong platform is built by adjusting to your specific market, your abilities, your audience, and your goals. Sometimes, platform building pays off immediately. Other times, the return on investment (ROI) is not obvious or immediate. Soon, you will be introduced to a very specific method to use to assess your results and make the next wise decision. It is known as "analytics," and I've included it so you can ensure that your actions are moving you closer to your goals at a reasonably quick pace.

In the many years I have been teaching and consulting individuals and companies on platform building, I have come to realize that some people should not do certain things, either because it scares them to do it or they have no natural aptitude for it. I believe you should pick the "low hanging fruit"—take what is easy for you and make it your primary strategy. Why not make driving customers to your business as simple and enjoyable as possible?

When you have implemented a few platform strategies and they are attracting lots of new business for you, come back and select a few more. You will be more skillful by then and have more clarity about what strategies are attracting the greatest number of new people to your business and bringing you the most money.

I started my first business when I was 15 years old in order to pay for college. I remember from harsh experience that in the beginning, there isn't always enough money to pay other people to do stuff you don't want to do. That is one reason why this book will be so incredibly helpful for you. When you apply these strategies, your revenues will increase and you'll be able to pay to delegate whatever you wish—and hand your new hire these step-by-step instructions to keep your platform going.

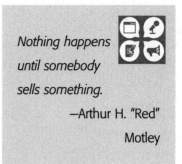

*Nothing happens until somebody sells something.*

—Arthur H. "Red" Motley

If you are a DIYer—by choice or by force—then in this book you will find the easiest, most complete, comprehensive "recipe book" to make sure you get the results you choose at any level you desire.

The thing is that you start. Today.

Your business is relying on you for its survival, and its life-blood is sales. Building a robust platform is the most interesting, effective, and sustainable way to attract lots of prospects and turn them into loyal, paying customers.

# Chapter 1

# What Is a Platform, and How Much Money Will It Make You?

If you are reading these words, your primary question about this book is likely to be, "What's in it for me?" That's exactly what your customers are asking also, before they invest their time or money in your product or service. It's a fair question and every purveyor should be grateful when someone stops to browse their wares.

So thank you. Thanks for trusting me this far and for giving this page a chance to let you know how keenly this book is designed to help you achieve your goals as a businessperson.

To sell you on reading these words, I have to guess why you picked it up in the first place. It's my job to determine what you hope to get from this and then to deliver it, so you will be a satisfied customer.

Here goes.

For us entrepreneurs, "growth" means "more sales." One way to get more sales is to get more new customers. More customers result from more people knowing about you, your product or your service. The way you get more people to know about you is by building your platform. "Platform" is a jargon word for a large, growing group of fans who love you, your product, or your service. Your platform is the crowd of people who want to buy your stuff.

When a famous person like Justin Bieber or Kim Kardashian sends a tweet about a product, service, or other artist they like, it usually goes viral. That's because all stars by definition have platforms.

You probably don't want to be chased by paparazzi or be on the cover of *People* magazine, but what could happen for you in your niche if everyone knew your business' name—or yours? How much more money will you make when lots of people realize you are the best purveyor of whatever you're selling? A sustainable, well-built platform will attract prospects to you with minimal effort. Your profits will increase at the same velocity as your platform grows.

It's time to grow your platform if:

- You want to grow your business by attracting new customers, clients, or patients.
- You have a new business you are trying to launch.
- Your sales are slumping—or never got off the ground.
- You want to introduce a new product or service to the market.
- You would like to attract investors or partners.
- You yearn to expand your brand.
- You are searching for new streams of revenue.
- You want to distinguish your career.
- You are being eaten alive by the competition.
- You are an author, artist, musician, designer, or other creative type looking to figure out how to make enough money to do what you love for a living.
- You are a speaker, coach, or consultant (or want to be), and you are putting your game plan together.
- You just want to make more money.

## WHO ARE THESE PEOPLE?

Just for the record, I use the word "customers" to refer to clients, patients, constituents, or listeners when referring to people who give you money or who take the action you want them to take. I use the word "money" to refer to whatever benefit it is that you desire from building your platform. Your goal may be "world peace" or "vote for me!" and I hope you achieve your goal, but we'll stick with "money" as a catchall term for now.

Done right, a platform becomes a prospect-generating machine—one that works for you 24/7 and never takes lunch breaks. It will enable you to touch and transform your customers in positive ways, whether that is as simple as an oil change or as significant as a life change.

## THE FUNDAMENTAL TRUTH ABOUT HUMANS

All humans are basically the same. This is true no matter where you go or when in history you encounter them, and no matter how you reach them tomorrow.

If you've been to Pompeii, a southern Italian city that was destroyed by a volcano in 79 A.D., you can actually see graffiti on the walls that says basically the same exact things as you see in graffiti today.

"The end is nigh!"

"Porteus is a jerk!"

"Buy bread from Avitus!"

That's because the human needs, interests, fears, and desires then were exactly the same as ours today. People want to be happy, healthy, and to live their lives in peace and abundance.

Your platform will flourish when you start to use this fundamental truth about all humans for your own good. We are all alike in this way: Everyone is primarily focused on his or her own life. People don't pay attention to things that do not immediately interest or affect them.

Are you allergic to cats? If you are, you're far more likely to notice cats in the environment than someone who is neutral about them.

Are you gluten intolerant? If so, you are a person who will actively look for potential gluten in anything you're about to eat, while the person you are sharing lunch with chomps into that sandwich without even thinking about it.

### FAMOUS AND REVERED SALES ADAGE

"To sell John Smith what John Smith buys, you must see John Smith through John Smith's eyes."

It is normal and natural for us to care about ourselves, our offspring, and our tribe. The best part of that fundamental truth?

To grow a business, all you need to do is to slip into the prospect's stream of consciousness. Tune into what they are tuned into: themselves. Show them how you, your product or your service will get them to their goals. With this alignment, you can make the right prospects take notice of what you've got. If it matches their goals, needs, or wants in that moment, you can get them to take action (give you their credit card).

The purpose of platform building is to attract as many qualified people as possible at the exact moment they are ready to buy. You want what is called "qualified traffic."

To summarize this entire book in a simple equation:

Platform = Traffic

Traffic = Money

therefore

Platform = Money

Get a platform, get money

A percentage of your traffic (flow of prospects) will always convert into customers who give you money. That means that the more and better-qualified traffic you get at the front end, the more money you get at the back end.

There's an art and a science to being in the right spot with the right message about the right product at the right time. Building a strong platform will allow you to attract lots of traffic, see what factors are converting browsers into buyers, winnow your best strategies down, and eventually, only spend resources like time and money where you will get the highest return on investment (ROI).

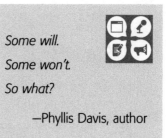

*Some will.*
*Some won't.*
*So what?*

—Phyllis Davis, author

Have you seen those guys who sell ice cream with pushcarts in the park on hot summer days? That's a decent business model. But when it rains, or during winter, they better switch to selling umbrellas or roasted chestnuts to keep the cash flowing in. They have to adapt to what their customers want, when they want it, and be smart enough to watch the signs. In this case, the "sign" means checking the weather before they set out for the day.

Now imagine some ambitious guy rolls up beside them with a super fancy pushcart that has flashing neon lights and pop music blaring from it. He invested a lot of money in appearances. This new guy is trying to sell life insurance policies to those same people strolling through the park. He looks great. He's getting a lot of attention. But how successful do you think he will be?

Exactly. Not so much. His timing and presentation are off. He may be getting attention, but it is not the right sort at the right time. He may be visible, but he is not converting (selling). A successful platform is based on market research, common sense, and timing. The parallel is someone who spends thousands foolishly marketing without first having taken time to gather relevant data to be certain the public will respond positively to his offering.

It's OK if you do not yet know where your customers are, much less the best way to reach them. We'll be doing some market research together in a few pages. A successful platform builds a "traffic attraction strategy" based on data, and also features a system of checks and balances that allows you to be sure your resources are being well-spent.

If you've already blown a lot of money on stuff that didn't work, take heart. That part of your learning curve just came to an end. You won't do that ever again.

Kevin M. owns an independent furniture store in Illinois. Seven years ago, he hired a small business-marketing consultant, who suggested he invest in radio advertising. He did and sure enough, sales went up. Kevin got too busy to pay attention, so he just kept right on advertising. A few years later, he decided to survey his customers. Was it the radio ad that had brought them in? Only one of the dozens of people he asked had even heard the radio ad! Kevin had been spending over $2,000 per month and that was not where his leads were coming from! He stopped the radio ads and his sales grew at the same rate they always had. When he figured out what really was driving growth, he was able put that extra $24,000+ per year into the right components. He just opened a

## THE STAGES OF PLATFORM BUILDING

**ONE**: The Planning Stage
- What should you do?
- What is easiest to do?
- What would success look like?
- Who is serving your people now?
- Are other businesses doing something you can adopt for yours?
- What resources are available to you?
- What will you need to learn to do?
- How much time can you/someone devote to analyzing test results?

**TWO**: The Learning and Setup Phase
- How do you set stuff up?
- When do you execute on it?
- Where do you put it?
- How do you do it?
- How do you prepare for good data collection?

**THREE**: The Testing Phase
- How do you know if it is working?
- Should you give it more time?
- What should you tweak?
- How do you interpret the metrics?

**FOUR**: The Optimization Phase
- What do you cut out?
- What do you tweak?
- How do you boost what's working?
- How do you introduce new strategies based on real time results?

**FIVE**: Repeat Phase
- Do more of what works by reinvesting some of your gross profits.
- Check in quarterly to be sure it is still working
- Slowly put more of your eggs in that basket
- Explore additional similar ways to reach the same group of people

second location recently. (We are going to talk about this matter in Chapter 3, "Analytics and Espionage," so you don't end up throwing your money away).

You may already know precisely where your customers are and just need some creative, innovative strategies to draw them out. If you are earlier in your business, you may need to do some conservative, controlled trial-and-error testing to find out who they are and how they think. Knowing who they are and where they are (geographically, emotionally, financially, etc.) will make your business run better for you. You will need to continue to do market research (data) using your common sense and testing the timing so you know your customer's habits.

## THE MYTH OF SALES

You may have heard this adage: "There are only two kinds of people in the world: those who know they are in sales, and those who don't."

Some people would be affronted to think they are "in sales." Somehow, sales seems like a profession that requires you to work in a used car lot wearing a thick gold chain and a floral polyester shirt unbuttoned halfway down your hairy chest.

### IF THE SHOE FITS, WEAR IT

If you were expecting a one-size-fits-all platform-building solution, one that promises you will make a million dollars in the next 30 days you are reading the wrong book. Here on Earth, things do not really work like that. A platform that is strong, sustainable, and smart is built on tried-and-true methods, one building block at a time. Sure, you or your product could become an "overnight sensation," and I hope that happens for you! But try not to be disappointed if it does not. Most things are not overnight sensations. You need to implement something, see if it is working, modify it if necessary, and try again.

In the words of my buddy Jeffrey Gitomer, sales trainer and author of many books including, *Jeffrey Gitomer's Little Red Book of Selling*, it is more like this: "Work your ass off for 15 years and poof! Instant success!"

Our goal in your case is to shave 12 to 14 years off Jeffrey's estimate.

The truth is, you've been using your selling skills—at whatever level you have them—since you first tried to get your mom to postpone your bedtime.

As a grown-up, you can use your sales skills to get people to hand you money for your product or service. (You don't have to rummage through used clothing shops for that disco shirt!) You are in sales any time you are trying to get another human being to take a definite action to give you something you want. Sales are how the world works. Improving your sales skills by deepening your ability to observe and predict human nature will help you to profit more from your platform and grow your business quicker.

## CUSTOMIZING YOUR PLATFORM

The easiest place to get started building your platform is to do what you are good at. Platform building can loosely be divided into three categories: personal appearances (appearing on television and radio, presenting in public, video blogging, etc.); writing (blog posts, articles, being quoted in other people's publications, writing ebooks); and strategy (pulling strings behind the scenes, organizing events, watching results, creating valuable relationships).

People tend to be good at doing things they enjoy. Once you have clarity about what that is for you, you will be able to choose more wisely.

To find out what your natural skills are as they relate to platform building, go to www.KellerMedia.com/BizQuiz and take the free, simple assessment there. You'll get an immediate result to help you know what strategies will be easiest for you personally to implement first.

The company I run now, Keller Media, Inc. (www.KellerMedia.com) is my sixth business. I began it in 1989 with a toddler, $150 saved from grocery money, a cardboard box for files and a gigantic Compaq computer my then-husband's company was going to throw away. I built it up to millions in revenue by doing what I was good at and what I could do, given time, money, and other responsibilities. If I can do this, so can you!

If you have a huge marketing team and a limitless budget, there will be a lot of street-smart marketing ideas you can learn in these pages. But if your business isn't launched yet or isn't profitable enough to afford a big marketing budget, in these pages you will find "bootstrap" methods. These methods will let you test out various ideas for cheap or for free whenever possible. I have used these methods myself and taught them to my clients (authors, speakers, consultants, coaches, and small business owners) for nearly 30 years. I've refined these methods to make them concise and the results clear and measurable. They are intended for you to use, adapt, and adopt.

## DO WHAT YOU'RE GOOD AT

What about the platform building strategies that you are not (yet) good at? Or the ones you don't have time to implement? Every small business owner has heard, "Do what you're good at and hire out the rest." But the truth is, nothing at all gets done if you aren't good at it, you dislike it, and you can't afford to hire out. The tasks just remain incomplete, frozen on your To Do list, which is an irony because if you implemented at least a few of these strategies to the best of your ability, you'd make the money to be able to afford to hire an expert to do the rest.

If you have ever read Michael Gerber's small-business classic, *The E-Myth*, you may recall the core principles of delegation. Gerber basically says, "Figure out how to do something. Then figure out how to do it more efficiently and successfully. Record your process exactly. Then delegate that perfected process to the lowest paid person who is capable of replicating it properly."

I recommend that you do not delegate any strategy in this book until you know how to work it and that it works for you and your business. (You don't want to be like Kevin running wasteful radio ads for his furniture store!) It is critical that you do these steps in order:

First, begin with crystal clarity about the people to whom you want to, plan to, or are currently selling your wares. Modern marketers call this "defining your avatars." When I consult clients on marketing their book, their business, or themselves as speakers, this is where we begin.

Commit to observing, analyzing, and recording the process of your upcoming growth spurt.

Next, analyze the source of the growth your business will be experiencing so you know which parts of your platform are producing the greatest results. This is called "analytics" and this is how you'll know if you're heading the right direction. (See Chapter 3 on Analytics on page 17).

So who are your avatars? All those nice people out there on the planet who are eager to give you their money just because you have exactly what they want or need.

# Chapter 2

# Creating a Customer Avatar

"Customer Avatar" is a marketing term for a composite picture of your average or ideal customer. If you are starting a new business, it's smart to begin by defining your ideal customer avatar. If you have data because you've been in business awhile, you can create more refined avatars based on what you know.

Knowing your customer avatar allows you to advertise, promote, and build your platform in the right places for the right people. It allows you to execute your strategy, monitor results, and adapt nimbly.

Defining your avatar is a result of gathering data, making smart guesses, and adjusting until you get it right. It is the process of paying attention to what is working so you can do more of it; and what isn't so you can stop doing it (or tweak it). This is called "analytics." (More on this in Chapter 3).

Analytics is where most overworked small-business owners fall into the black hole of marketing—like Kevin from the last chapter did with his furniture store, running radio ads that cost money but netted little. He forgot to see if it was working. The more you know about what your avatar wants, values, and needs, the more easily you'll be able to connect with them, sell to them, and not spend your platform-building time and money stuck in box canyons.

Here are a few of the questions you will be able to answer once you know your avatars:

- What format of content (online, video, display ads, print articles, etc.) is most likely to reach my ideal customer?
- What words, colors, language, and images are most likely to attract these people to me?
- What type of story should my marketing message be sharing?
- What are my customers paying attention to already?
- What are my customer's trigger points?
- When will they be ready to buy?
- What makes them buy?
- What do they value?
- Where are they?

In traditional marketing, these facts are called "demographics" (age, gender, etc.) and "psychographics" (how people think, what colors they like best, the kinds of movies they prefer, etc.). Because a list of character traits is hard to conceptualize and keep in mind, modern marketers use these facts to assemble what is known as an "avatar"—a composite of a typical customer. A business may have several different avatars. It becomes easier to write marketing copy, choose the right images for an ad, decide what sort of bonus would appeal most to them, and in general formulate ideas that will appeal to that specific avatar when you know "who" that person is.

## AVATAR DATA POINTS

Obviously, no one avatar will account for all the traits. We have four at my company. They are the ideal client, the good enough client, the person willing to learn but who cannot yet be represented as talent, and the person we do not want to work with under any circumstances.

Depending on your product or service, some things to consider when assembling your customer avatars include the following data:

- Age
- Race
- Gender
- Household income
- Hobbies
- Profession
- Marital status

- Parental status
- Music preferences
- Pet lover
- Allergies
- Culinary preferences
- Leisure activities
- Exercise preferences
- Travel choices
- Financial anxiety
- Amount of time spent online
- Own or rent

Now that you're looking behind the scenes, you likely realize that you've been asked questions like these by businesses for years; you just didn't recognize what was going on.

Obviously, the information you want to use to create your own avatars will depend on your product or service. If you run a restaurant, you want one set of stats; if you make fancy pet accessories, you want to know other things. When it becomes easy to imagine your avatars, they will become your invisible beta testers.

So where do you get these stats?

If you are just starting out in business, block out an hour. Take a notebook and a pen to a quiet place that inspires you. Turn off your cell phone, disconnect, and really think. Who are you building your product for? People like you? What kinds of customers would you really like? Who do you see eating your restaurant's food, buying your sculptures, or reading your book?

## ARE YOU TOO FAR AHEAD OF THE CURVE?

A business that opens a Korean-Mexican-Caribbean fusion restaurant at high prices might be in trouble if their ideal avatar is adventurous, well-off foodies, especially if the restaurant is located in a place where most residents prefer all-you-can-eat buffets and fast food.

If you intend to succeed in a regional business, developing your avatar before you lease a location could help you make sure you don't end up fighting an uphill battle.

If you have a team or a spouse who is tuned in to your business adventure, ask him or her to join you in the brainstorming or to look over what you devised.

If you are in an established business, start defining your avatars with the easiest one: the client from hell. What is a composite of the people you have least enjoyed serving? The ones who threatened lawsuits because their coffee was cold; the ones who are always suspicious that you're going to do something underhanded; the ones who ended up taking 20 times more energy than the profitable ones? I recommend you read Perry Marshall's book *80/20 Sales and Marketing* for help figuring out the math behind why you want to identify this type and avoid this avatar in the future.

Then work on the avatars that have been most profitable for your company so far. If these people do not match the ideal avatars you thought you might attract when you opened the business, is it too late? Can you still get those people, too? Are you in the right market, with the right product?

## BUILD A PHOTO ALBUM OF YOUR AVATARS

In modern marketing, companies often develop an actual "data sheet" for each of their avatars and even attach a photo of someone who represents what that person might look like (see Figure 2-1 on page 15). List the relevant characteristics from the data points you gathered to describe your avatar. Imagine this person. What do they look like? How do they dress? Then give their avatar names like "Evan the Entrepreneur" or "Cindy Montgomery, Fitness Fanatic."

### HOW TO USE YOUR AVATARS

While visualizing your avatar, ask yourself what she or he would think about the following points.

- Would my avatar use these keywords and key phrases?
- Is this product moving my avatar to like and trust me?
- Is this product setting the right image for my avatar?
- Is this product meeting my avatar's needs easily?
- Am I providing the best solution for my avatar?
- What other choices does my avatar have?

# Jon Marsh

Age: 43

Married to Courtney for 14 years

Two kids, ages 11 and 9

Lives in a suburb

Has a Bachelor's

Financially pressured

- ❖ Realizes he needs to make more money to secure his family's future
- ❖ Probably the first born child or from a family of high achievers
- ❖ Still establishing his place in the world, in his own mind
- ❖ Imagines himself bringing in a lot more money as a speaker
- ❖ May have some speaking – but not paid (much) per event
- ❖ Strong drive to do a book for career or business benefits
- ❖ No time to focus on interpersonal relationships in business
- ❖ Stark division between personal and business life
- ❖ Will execute precisely but gets frustrated easily
- ❖ Believes he is exceptionally intelligent
- ❖ Highly tech savvy
- ❖ Driven

**FIGURE 2–1.** Sample Avatar Data Sheet

It may sound simplistic, but armed with the names of these "people" and a clear identity for each of them, you (and your team) can spend your time thinking about what Evan or Cindy might think of the packaging you are considering for your new product. Would Evan care if it was in a recyclable box? Would Cindy? Would Evan be interested in a pedometer that also reminds him of important meetings he has that day? Would Cindy? Which blog title would most appeal to Cindy's deepest needs? What does Evan think about while he's shaving?

Print color copies and give one to everyone who will be involved in marketing or selling to these people. Keep a set on your desk, where you can see them. Before you publish that next blog post, chase a media outlet, plan a promotion, or paint your store a new color, ask yourself, "Would my avatar be drawn to this?"

Many high-level marketing consultants get paid thousands of dollars to help companies define their avatars, but you've just been taught the basics for free! Now that you know who you want to attract to your business, you'll want a system to empirically determine if the methods you are about to employ to attract them are actually effective. We're ready for analytics.

# Chapter 3

# Analytics and Espionage

Did you like math in school? I didn't, but I sure do like it now.

As entrepreneurs, math becomes a beautiful thing because now it is tied to money. How much you bring in (gross profit) gets reduced by what it costs you to attract that money (cost of doing business), which results in the cherished number that represents what you get to keep (your net profit).

Funny how such a thorny subject in fourth grade can become a thing of beauty as an adult, huh?

Platform building is all about increasing your gross profit by easily attracting more customers to your business while lowering the cost of customer acquisition, so that your net profit burgeons.

"Analytics" refers to what percentage of a population of your suspected avatars actually buys from you. Your analytics will guide you quickly to increased clarity on your avatars, on what marketing is attracting them, and therefore how many people you have to reach to earn a profit.

Here are two examples to help you understand analytics.

## Scenario One

You decide to buy Google ads. You pay Google $10 every time someone clicks on your website link. (The real cost of a click on Google varies based on many factors). Out of every 20 clicks, one person buys.

Your analytics: $10 per click x 20 clicks = $200 per one sale

This makes your "customer acquisition cost" from Google ads $200 per sale. If your customer is buying something that costs $201 or more, you're good. If they are not, you will find yourself looking for a day job pretty quickly.

### Scenario Two

You run highly targeted Google ads based on what you think you know about your customer avatar. These ads are more expensive, because a lot of other companies have a similar avatar. So these ads actually cost you $15 per click, which is 50 percent more than in scenario one.

But because you have been working on the avatar model, you are better at creating attractive ads. That's why this time, out of every 20 clicks, 6 people buy.

Your analytics: $15 per click x 20 clicks = $300 total spent
$300/6 sales = $50 per sale

In scenario two, you have reduced your cost of customer acquisition by 75 percent, even though you are spending more per click. Both scenarios involve analytics. The second scenario tells you that you are smarter now about who you throw your marketing dollars toward. This is the value of analytics. Even though it's more per click, it costs less per sale, and that's what matters most.

## THE REAL COST OF ADVERTISING

Advertising costs are calculated like this:

Cost of the ad development + Cost of the placement

For instance, if you hire a graphic designer to make a "pretty" ad, whether it is a display ad for your local paper, for *The New York Times*, or for your next Facebook post, you incur that cost. If you are also paying someone to write your ad (your employee, a copywriter) that is an additional cost. If you are writing your ads (or blogs, other marketing copy) yourself, then your hourly rate is what you're paying.

And that's only the first half of the equation!

The second half is the cost of placement. Are you paying a magazine or newspaper or website to place your ad in their publication? Are you running a Google, Twitter or Facebook campaign online and paying one of those companies to show your ad to people using their service?

Your job as your own marketing director (until you can afford to hire one) is to stay aware of this: are you earning more from your ads than you are investing in preparing and placing them?

For example, a disheartened author wrote me recently to tell me her sad news. She said she had taken the advice I'd given at one of my webinars and begun blogging twice a week as a way to test the interest her ideal avatars actually have in her book. Problem is, she's been blogging for more than a year and has gotten almost no response from the handful of people who are even reading her blogs. She wasn't doing her analytics.

She should have taken the low response/engagement rate with her blogs as a sign that something is wrong:

- with her writing,
- her topic,
- her marketing,
- her images,
- her timing,
- her credibility, or
- her core subject matter.

A year of blog posts twice a week is 104 posts (52 weeks x 2). Assuming it takes her 30 minutes to an hour to write, find graphics for and post each one, she's put in between 52 and 104 hours doing this.

If she even worked for the average U.S. minimum wage of just $7.25, that's $377 to $754 lost. If all her blogging didn't even directly attract that much in profits, then she's working below the minimum wage!

She's obviously doing something wrong. In her case, her writing is fuzzy, and her only product is a $25 ebook. She's sold three. That's far too expensive for an ebook by an unknown author with no credentials.

Is her blogging paying off? No. Of course, now she's emotionally committed to blogging after a year of doing it. Should she stop cold? Should she rethink? Should she continue in frustration?

One must boldly look at the ROI (return on investment) from any advertising or marketing activity. Analytics helps you objectively answer the question: is this working for me?

## BLOGGING FOR ANALYTICS

Blogging is a great way to start listening to what does and doesn't appeal to your avatars. It is a relatively slow but inexpensive method of aggregating analytic data. You likely already have a website or a public page on Facebook for your business. Let's estimate that it takes you 45-60 minutes to write a blog, select its image, and post it. You write three blogs a week because someone told you that's the recommended frequency. When you see one of your blogs getting a 50 percent better response (Likes, comments, retweets, etc.) than your other blogs, you wisely decide to boost that post to your avatars on Facebook. (These are the people Facebook notices are most attracted to your stuff so far). You choose to invest $20 every time you boost a posted blog ono Facebook (see Chapter 10, "Social Media"). Use Figure 3–1 to track what your posts are costing. At the end of three months of experimental blogging and boosting, what have you learned? Did you make any sales? Did you get measurably more hits on your website? Did you get more inquiries? Can these things be traced back to the blog posts?

If you answered yes, then you're doing fine! Continue modifying your blogs to get closer and closer to becoming irresistible to your avatar. Notice what words, format, subjects, headlines, tone of voice, and writing style get the best responses online and replicate them. This is priceless marketing data that will help you craft sales copy and engage more avatars going forward.

---

## Quarterly Blogging Cost Worksheet

If you boost one out of every 12 posts to Facebook, then your investment in 12 posts is:

12 hours x your estimated hourly wage:         $_____

The $20 boost on Facebook:         $____20_____

Subtotal:         $_____

It typically takes 3 to 6 months of attentive, thoughtful, adaptive blogging before you figure out what your avatars' hot buttons are—what makes them click on your offer, your website, your webinar, your buy page, or come into your shop. So to figure out how much this Facebook boost costs over a three-month period:

Subtotal above:         $_____

Multiplied by three months

Your total investment in blogging for three months:         $_____

---

**FIGURE 3–1.** Blog Post Cost Worksheet

If you answered no, then you're not doing so well. You want to immediately use the ultimate marketing three-pack.

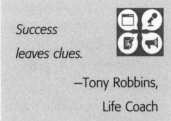

*Success leaves clues.*

—Tony Robbins, Life Coach

### Implement + Observe + Adapt

There's a solution to less than stellar results from any marketing foray. True blue-blood marketers tell you to "test everything." Only a fool would disagree, but what the marketers mean is that you—as a busy small-business owner who probably dreams of working fewer than ten hours a day—should test every marketing piece for:

- The colors
- The images
- The headline
- The body copy
- The time of day the content runs
- The placement of the content
- The audience you selected

And on and on. Those marketers are 100 percent right. Absolutely! Yes, you should do all that for every page on your website, post, blog, ad, article, pitch, sales letter, marketing campaign, and everything else you will ever create for your business.

Yep. Good luck with that.

Did your eyes roll to the back of your head when you even thought about all the work it is to gather analytics and test, test, test? Mine do, too.

I will tell you a secret: I still can't bring myself to test all this stuff. Who has the time?

So I've devised a much easier way for you to do the critically important work of analytics. I call it "Analytics Light." It derives from the well-known saying "Success Leaves Clues." I'll split it up for a product-based business and a service-based business, to make it even easier for you.

## ANALYTICS LIGHT FOR A PRODUCT-BASED BUSINESS

The easiest way to figure out if anyone is going to buy your product is to spend a chunk of time doing online research. Invest a couple of hours up front and a) you'll get to skip some of the onerous brain-scrambling testing stuff we just talked about and b) you'll get better results right from the start.

Take some time to find out:

- Is anyone selling anything like your product?
- How many units do you estimate they are selling each month?
- How much are they charging? Is shipping free?
- How is it wrapped?
- What do their store displays look like?
- How much foot traffic do they get in their location?
- Which competitor is the most successful in your space?
- For retail, what do their stores look like? How is their parking? Is their staff pleasant? Is the place well-lit and clean?
- How many people walk out with a purchase?
- What kinds of comments are they getting on social media about their service or their product?
- What can you learn about your customers from this research?

Much of this can be obtained by checking out the website of a digital store, too. Buy or order the object from your competitor(s) and see if they have good quality, good customer service, and an easy ordering process. When you get it, note how it is packaged, if it was delivered on time, and then return it. What is their return process like? If you saw any glitches in that process, it's a big flashing sign that your business can eat some of their market share by doing it better! As a pseudo-customer for a product similar to yours, you know intimately what "good" is. Use this information to your own advantage.

## ANALYTICS LIGHT FOR A SERVICE-BASED BUSINESS

Are you offering a "quiet" service delivered in your office, like an attorney or a psychologist? Or are you offering a service you bring to your customer, like a landscaper or a handyman?

Your competitors are not just "people in the same kind of service business," but proprietors of all service businesses that are doing well. Check out successful service providers in other industries: plumbers, dog groomers, home healthcare delivery businesses. Are any of them doing something spectacular that you could incorporate into your strategy?

Choose who you will "stalk" by finding the ones who have the highest Yelp.com rating. Then find out:

- Where are your competitors geographically?
- What do their offices look like?
- What methods do they use to deliver the service?
- What do they charge?

- Are their websites professional looking?
- How many of them are in your area, if relevant?
- Check the parking lot, if relevant—what kinds of cars do their customers drive?
- Do the customers you see leaving their office look like the people you pictured as your avatars?
- Trail their service trucks. What kinds of neighborhoods are their customers in?
- Make an appointment—how long do you have to wait to get into your appointment? How are you treated? Is their phone service professional?
- If it is an online service business, how responsive are they to your emails if you ask an anonymous question through their contact form?
- Do they offer anything extra, beyond what you planned to offer?
- Stake out their location, if applicable. Pretend you're a private investigator for an hour (trench coat and cigar optional). What do you see going on?

Your competitors are saving you many hours and lots of money by broadcasting how to do things successfully. "Success leaves clues." Why waste your own money and time when it is so much easier to do a little espionage? This will let you see how other successful people are doing it. Then you can test and improve on their methods.

## CORPORATE ESPIONAGE 101

Almost every business has a website.

Type in keywords (see the Glossary for definitions of the marketing jargon) for your product or service on Google or another search engine. Whose websites come up on the first page? Consumers rarely go to the second page, so websites listed after page one are not doing much good for their owners. Ignore them.

Write down the URLs of every website on the first page and exactly which keywords and key phrases you used to find them. Use them for your own site later—simple to do, but if you are nervous, ask your webmaster to do it for you. There are different ways to ask the same thing. Type it in the way that seems natural to you, but also consider other peoples' ways of phrasing things.

For example, consider these key phrases and their alternates:

- "Where do I find a good CPA?" vs. "Highest Rated CPA in Atlanta"
- "Fiberglass fishing boat" vs. "Best fishing boat"
- "Best baby stroller" vs. "Blue baby strollers"

Although the searcher may be looking for exactly the same thing in these examples, the search phrases are critically different. Google will bring up what it "thinks" is closest to what the person wants.

When you notice that people use a term or phrase for your product or service that is different than what seems right or natural to you, who cares? This is a perfect example of "the customer is always right." Use the words that the majority of people use, even if you disagree with their phrasing, their spelling, or their mistakes. Surely, you've mistyped a word during a Google search and had something unexpected pop up. (If not, just type "Goo" when you intend to type "Google" and you'll see what I mean!) There are clever people making money by having keywords and key phrases that are based on common mistakes.

*Warning*: If your biggest competitors do not show up when you use the keywords you think are "right," before you congratulate yourself on your genius, check again. It likely means you are simply choosing different key words in your search. If you are also using the less popular words on your website, change them there too. It doesn't matter who is right—it matters that you get paid.

### What Words Are Your Competitors Using?

Go deeper. Next, on a computer running Windows, go to or each of the competitor websites that are listed on the first page of Google when you search. Right click and select "View Source." Look for the lines of code near the top that say:

**<meta name= "keywords" content=**

Read the words that come after this. Google doesn't use these words to search anymore, but they are still helpful because other search engines do.

**<meta name= "description" content=**

This is gold! Write these words down verbatim and use them as a model.

This is where your competitors' special words are hidden—even though they themselves may not even know they are there! Does this seem like corporate espionage? It is! Go back again and enter these new and improved keywords to search Google, Twitter, Facebook, Bing, and other popular search engines. What other competitors does this lead you to? What do their websites look like? How can you use this information to your own competitive advantage?

## IS IT WORKING?

*Warning*: Even if something is working great for your competitor, it may not work the same for you. Or it may not work at all for you, for any number of reasons. This is why you always want to keep an eye on those analytics. Remember: "See if it is working."

- Is the blog on Topic A getting more likes on Facebook than Topic B?
- Is being interviewed on local radio shows actually bringing in any new customers?
- Are more people reading your LinkedIn articles after work or during work hours?
- Do more people click when you use headline one or headline two?
- And of course, are you making more net profit this month than last month?

## THE PRINCIPLE OF ONE THOUSAND

If a thousand people have seen your ad, read your blog, been sent your offer, signed up for your newsletter, watched your video on YouTube, and none of them have given you money, you've got a problem. It's time to do some rethinking and some retooling. You need to fix a leak in your marketing pipes somewhere.

If a few of them have taken the desired action, at least you've got something to work with. The marketing term for how many people take action on any marketing overture is called "conversion." You can build your whole business marketing from now until the day you sell your company by focusing on just this one strategy!

But first, you need to know how to get at least 1,000 people to see anything.

### Split Testing

Split testing basically means you split something in half and test one element against the other, so you can see which performs better.

One half of any marketing piece (a blog, a Facebook ad, a display ad, a product package, a web page, etc.) could have a different headline, image, color, offer, or phrasing than the other half. Take your budget for driving traffic to that piece and split that in half. Put 50 percent of your budget on each half, drive 500 people to each half, and pick the winner out of those thousand people.

Did "A" bring in seven new customers, but "B" brought in ten? "A" is a dud. Dump that loser!

Now, since you have one working and we like the fact it brought ten new customers, keep it going, but test against it. Three-fourths or 75 percent of your marketing money should continue to go to "B," the winning half because that one works. One-fourth or 25 percent of your marketing money should now go to a new, better version—version "C."

Now drive a thousand people to each.

How's that working? Did "B" keep the lead, or did "C" shock you and although it naturally took longer to get a thousand people to see "C," because it had just a quarter of your budget, did it convert 10 or 12 new customers? If yes, then a star is born!

If the 25 percent converts better than the original (test) ad/blog/whatever, then you make it the new base, give it 75 percent of your budget and then run a different 25 percent test against it.

Repeat.

You can keep on doing this until you're 106 years old. You can also stop whenever you decide you don't need any more money than you're making now.

This is a genius idea because it greatly minimizes your risks. I got the seed of this idea from my pal, the world-renowned marketing guru Jay Abraham. It works every time, and protects you from losing a lot of money. Best of all, it helps you quickly make a lot of money.

## What to Test

Marketers know that the headline makes all the difference. In an email, the subject line determines if people will open it up. In a blog or video, the title determines if they will consume it. You can do a split test on any and all elements you desire. The great news is now that you know the method for conversion testing and that one thousand is considered a fair test, you are bullet proof. All you need is one winner, and then every split test after that, you will be testing something successful against something that might be more successful. This will help you get great results faster.

Success comes down to positioning. Analytics is how you find exactly the right position for your business.

# Chapter 4

# The Power of Positioning

In their seminal book, *Positioning*, Al Ries and Jack Trout wrote, "Positioning is not what you do to a product. Positioning is what you do in the mind of a prospect. That is, how you position the product in the mind of the prospect."

Do you want to be "the low-price leader" or do you want to be a boutique serving high-end clients? Do you want to be like Chuck E. Cheese or some swanky candlelit restaurant? Everything about your marketing message, your image and your appearance should reinforce your positioning decisions.

Appearances matter. Do you look like the kind of person (online, in person, on your website, in the shipping box they open, in your store) that your avatars want to do business with? If you hire a new babysitter and she shows up to watch your toddler in a prom dress and heels, how confident are you going to feel about leaving your child with her? If you hire some scruffy handyman with a stained, torn shirt over his big belly, who comes rattling up your driveway in his beat-up creepy old van, you likely hired him because he's cheap, even though you'll want to bleach everything he touched when he leaves. There's no right or wrong here, but once you make a choice, you'll want to "build to suit."

Positioning means showing up like the person the customer wants and expects you to be.

Ford Saeks, who owns www.PrimeConcepts.com and who is also an impactful small-business marketing trainer and consultant, told me, "Business first impressions are critical to setting the stage for trust and credibility. People make their decisions about whether they're going to do business with you in less than three seconds."

If you want to position yourself as a legitimate player in the minds of your customers, you need to look, act, walk, and talk the part.

If you drive people to your business because you've built your marketing platform, but their first impression of your website, parking lot or lobby is that you are unkempt, not trustworthy, disorganized, low-end, grubby, or suspicious, you will have wasted your work attracting them. People are highly unlikely to ever give you a second chance.

A few years into running Keller Media, I decided to move the company to larger quarters. We were growing so fast, and I was working so many hours, I didn't have time to ponder decorating issues. Besides, we didn't get that many visitors. For the first time, I had a huge office all my own. I asked the movers to place two mismatched armchairs in my private seating area. One of them accidentally broke a leg off one of the armchairs, so I told them to just prop it against the wall. Seemed like a fine idea at the time.

About three months later, the CEO of a major public company came to meet with me. He was deciding between me and another literary agent. I really wanted to handle his book. He would have been a perfect feather in my cap.

He arrived by limo. He met my courteous, efficient team and then I led him into my office for tea and a chat. He chose the armchair settled against the wall. Our conversation was going great until he suddenly decided to pull his chair a little closer to the coffee table . . .

And he instantly toppled over, ankles in the air!

He was gone within a minute. I trailed him to his limo apologizing profusely. He never spoke to me again. Lesson learned. I was penny wise and pound foolish. I had figured "someday" I would buy all new office furniture. I thought it was virtuous to start at the bottom and claw my way up. I was wrong.

I should have made sure that both my office and I looked the part if I wanted to succeed. I lost a considerable amount of money because that client left, and I might have had a lawsuit on my hands if he had hurt more than his pride.

Can you afford to start at the top—or even close to it? I asked Ford, "What if someone can't afford to look like an A-list player, and they think they'll make the money first and then..."

Ford replied, "Sell their car, their TV set, whatever. There's really nothing more important than their image. You have to walk before you can run. Of course you have to be able to work within the means of your budget, but whatever kind of budget you have, you can still improve your image . . . there's always a way to get it done if you're really serious about it."

What kind of image are you projecting for your product, service, business, team, and yourself? What position are you claiming in your client's mind?

Jeff Hayzlett is the host and chairman of C-Suite TV, the former CMO of Kodak, and the author of *Think Big, Act Bigger*. In his book, he discusses the psychology of positioning yourself—in your customer's mind and in your own.

Jeff believes, "You've got to play big to win big. People believe what they see, so you need to look the part, act the part, talk the part." I've known him most of my career and seen him grow. Today, he is the picture of supreme success and confidence, and as a direct result, he does business deals with huge national companies for large sums of money. Does your image match what the kind of people you want to do business with are expecting?

I asked Jeff, "Was there ever a time in your life when you were afraid or just starting out or not quite certain? You come across as incredibly 100 percent confident. Do you still have moments of fear? How do you handle them? How do you pull yourself back up to say, 'Okay, this is what I'm going to do'? What's the emotional strategy you use?"

"Let's be clear," Jeff said. "Every human being has fear. Every entrepreneur, every business owner, every Wall Street officer has fear. The key is that the real successful people have learned to push through it. We realize it only lasts for a few seconds."

"It's like being on the high dive or the first time you ever asked the woman who became your wife to go out with you when you were first dating. You're petrified, you're absolutely petrified. I'm 6 foot 3, 370 pounds, and I was petrified of a 5-foot-1 woman. That's the reason why we got to where we're at as a species: because eons ago, one of our ancestors in the human evolution chain was more scared than the other guy and ran faster. It's ingrained in us. Fear is innate in us, so it's a natural feeling. The issue is you've got to step through it."

I asked Jeff about his strategy. He said, "I tell myself 'No one's gonna die.' In everything that we do in life, outside of operating heavy machinery, race car driving or performing surgery, chances are that in most of the stuff we do in business every day, no one's gonna die. If you know that most of your [business] decisions are based on that fact, what's your problem with going for it?"

Fran Tarkenton made a great comment when he was the keynote speaker at a convention Jeff attended in 1986. Jeff recalls Tarkenton saying, "If you haven't lain awake at night as an entrepreneur wondering how you're going to make payroll the next day, you haven't lived. Many of us live a lot. Which means we risk, we take chances and we're fearful, but no one's gonna die."

In *How to Stop Worrying and Start Living*, a classic by Dale Carnegie, we are taught a genius strategy for getting through fear in business and in life. He taught me to ask myself, "What is the worst that could possibly happen here?" And then, "Can I live with that?" This clears our minds so we can answer the question, "OK, what can I do to make sure that doesn't happen?"

Not everything you do to build your platform will appeal to everyone. Reality indicates that whatever you implement from this book is likely to need some tweaking before it starts generating the kind of results you seek. That's just life. I'm given you proven strategies to minimize your risk, things you can split test to perfection. How brave can you be? After all, no one's gonna die.

You have to bravely try, test, adapt, and develop your strategies until you find the one(s) that produce the best results for the least input of resources (time, money, staff). A well-built platform will position your product or service in the minds of the people who are most likely to buy it.

Because that's what it all comes down to: people.

## THE GOLDEN RULE OF LIKE AND TRUST

People do business with people they like and trust—even if they have never met them or if they only know them by their online reputation. You may think you "know" Madonna, Brad Pitt, Richard Branson, or Barack Obama, but in reality, you do not. You know what they want you to see—their public image. You know only what they have shown to the public. And yet, you have an opinion about them and what kind of person they are. Are they reckless and wild? Brilliant? Ignorant? You have an opinion about a person who is a total stranger! You have judged her or him based on the scantiest information.

Your current and future clients are doing the exact same thing about you. This is a factor many business owners overlook.

You want to transition people from browsers into customers, and customers into loyal, raving fans—people who are passionate enough to recommend you to their friends. They may even defend you if someone says something negative. They think about you when they are looking for your product or service. They are *favorably disposed* toward you.

Why does this matter?

Who the heck cares what other people think of you?

You may dance to the beat of a different drummer and may be darn proud that you do. Fine.

Except for this fact: People do business with people they like and trust.

Your platform is a way to let them get to know you—that you are trustworthy, competent, honorable, and likable.

We have to think of these future clients as friends. The poet William Butler Yeats (1923, Nobel Prize for Literature) said, "There are no strangers here. Only friends you have not yet met."

When you become likable (even just in your public persona—you can be a grizzled misanthrope in private life), you create a buzz. It helps, of course, if you really do like people. Your ability to create a compelling, engaging, growing platform will develop because of your ability to play nice, make friends, and share. That is probably stuff you learned in kindergarten and have used every day since. You will be fine. You can do this.

## WHAT YOUR PLATFORM WILL DO FOR YOU

According to Ries and Trout in the book, *Positioning*, "The mind, as a defense against the volume of today's communications, screens and rejects much of the info offered to it. In general, the mind accepts only what matches prior knowledge or experience." For example:

- How many airlines do you have to choose from? Which do you prefer and why?
- How many restaurants can you drive to right now? Yet where do you go most often?
- How many types of mustard are for sale in your grocery store? Which do you usually buy?

Helping your clients prefer you is done by first attracting them with a strong, clear USP (unique selling proposition), then wooing them through things like good service, quality products or services, and great people giving them a great experience.

We are flooded with choice. We are lambasted hourly by an unprecedented number of messages that imply your life is not good enough without a certain product, weight, look, garment, or service. A strong platform will heighten your ability to reach out to your customer through the chaos and say, "Here, take my hand. I have the right solution for you, and I will present it in a way that gets you the result you crave in the easiest, fastest, most effective way possible" That is valuable to people.

Platform building will help you get your message heard despite the noise in their heads.

When I first began in sales, the adage was "five hits makes the sale." That meant that in order to get a stranger to notice that you exist (you = you, your product, or your

## WHAT'S A USP?

A "USP" is your unique selling proposition, stated as clearly and succinctly as humanly possible. Here are some examples:

- "Spectacular Ideas. Exceptional People. Extraordinary Results" (that's ours)
- "The low-price leader"
- "We try harder"
- "The Relentless Pursuit of Perfection"

These indicate each company's USPs. They allude to what makes them special in the marketplace. What's yours going to be?

service) you have to wiggle it in front of their noses five times. Now, some sales gurus say, "Seven hits makes the sale." That is because of the consumer bombardment.

Our customers are so overwhelmed with messages that it is easy to overwhelm or annoy them. How can you possibly be heard above the noise? By giving the right people the right message at the right time. That's how you attract customers. But unless you specialize in tourists, you probably want repeat business. That's where deciding to create a sustainable business comes in.

# Chapter 5

# Planning a Sustainable Business

The strategies in this book will help you attract new clients in endless supply: that is the big result of platform building. But if your new customers find out there is just a man (or woman) and not a wizard behind the green curtain, they are going to flee Oz as fast as they came.

In the old days, before online rating places like www.Yelp.com, www.TripAdvisor.com, www.OpenTable.com, and even www.RateMyProfessors.com and www.HealthGrades.com, the worst that would happen if a company or service provider dished out poor goods or lousy service is that they would get a bad reputation. Maybe they would even have to fold.

We can see remnants of these phenomena in the over-priced restaurants that cling like parasites to tourist areas year after year despite the poor quality of their food or service, simply because of the fact that no one comes there twice and they do not need repeat business.

You probably do want repeat business and a good reputation—online and via word-of-mouth. Consumers have more choices today than ever, and they vote with their dollars. One truly furious customer who deploys an aggressive social media lambasting campaign can do serious damage.

Michael Glauser is the executive director of Jeffrey D. Clark Center for Entrepreneurship in the John M. Huntsman School of Business in Salt Lake City, Utah, an entrepreneur, business consultant, and the author of *Main Street Entrepreneur: Build Your Dream Company Doing What You Love Where You Live*. Michael rode his bike around the U.S. interviewing entrepreneurs. His perspective on entrepreneurship resonated with me in a recent conversation.

Michael explained, "One hundred years ago, we had an agricultural economy, which meant that most of us were in food production and distribution. That is where all the jobs were."

Next came the industrial revolution. Michael explains that the people who could produce the most products fastest were the most successful companies. Customers had to buy whatever was produced. Everyone has heard Henry Ford's famous saying, "You can buy my cars in any color you want as long as they are black."

> *If you do not build that community of really loyal followers who love you, then people are going to constantly be looking for features and benefits, and comparing products.*
>
> —Michael Glauser

Next came the information economy. Computers, cell phones, satellites and so on. Many people today are in the information business, moving information around and getting paid for it.

"Right now, we're in what I call the 'customer economy,'" Michael said. "There are more products and services in the market than ever before, and there are more variations of brands within each of those product lines. The customers are kind of keen. They can buy whatever they want, wherever they want, and they can get it for a great price. They can get it customized, and they get it personalized. This new customer economy is all about building communities of people that love you, love your products, love your service, and have chosen you as their provider."

Growing a sustainable business comes down to whether or not you can satisfy customers—even wow them—when they interact with you. Attracting customers to you with a great platform is the easy part. Winning them over as your loyal customers so they do not think of going anywhere else is the sustainability factor.

For example, I have had a Capital One® credit card for 15 years. I originally got it because they do not charge foreign transaction fees, and I travel outside the U.S. often enough to make that a valuable feature. One of the main reasons I stay with them, though, has nothing to do with my travel schedule. When I call for help, the people who answer the phone are in the U.S. and speak excellent English. I find this is expedient, to not have to ask, "What?" and "Could you please say that again?" while I'm trying to solve a simple customer service transaction. (This is not a comment against those individuals for whom English is not their native language! I speak passable Italian but not well enough that I should be employed in a customer service role in Italy.)

Oddly, my long relationship with Capital One means I smile with a sense of ownership when I see those, "What's in your wallet?" commercials. How weird is that? I give them money, and yet I feel like I have some role in their success. I just wrote two complimentary paragraphs about them, and they do not even actually know I exist as a person. But I've come to like and trust them, all based on a few positive telephone interactions I have had with the customer service person in the time I have been their customer.

The moral of the story? It does not take a whole lot more effort to make customers happy.

You as a business owner (even if your "business" is just you and your book, your song, your speech, or your tax accounting services!) have the opportunity to go not the whole extra mile, but just the extra few inches it takes to go from "typical" to "terrific."

## MICHAEL GLAUSER'S "FOUR LEVELS OF CUSTOMER SERVICE"

On his bike tour, Michael Glauser saw that the levels of customer service determine who gets the most customers (and thus the biggest profits).

- *Level One*. You just tolerate your customers. You and your staff do the minimum, providing the basics as inexpensively as possible and with the least hassle for you.
- *Level Two*. You meet their expectations. They expect certain things when they patronize your business. If you deliver the goods, they will say, "Yes, I'm satisfied." The problem is, according to Michael, they are not "loyal."
- *Level Three*. You exceed their expectations. You have figured out what they are really looking for when they come to you. You have strategized and determined what more you can give, so when your customers complete a transaction with you, as they walk away they say, "Wow! That is a phenomenal company. No one else treats me like that."
- *Level Four*. Treating customers as partners. You actually engage them in your business. You find a core group of connected, happy customers. Then you go to them and say, "I would like to meet your needs at the highest level. Will you work with me to help design this product or this service? I will make sure it meets your needs exactly. I will give you significant discounts over time if you work with me on some beta tests of this product."

You actually kind of co-op them into the development of your products or services. Then the minute that product hits the marketplace, you already have people who have said, "I am going to buy that!" Maybe people have even bought it before you get it to the marketplace. That way, you do not really launch anything until you know people really want it. (This reduces your risk!)

This is one of the things that sites like Kickstarter or Indiegogo have done well. According to Michael, "They have allowed you to float out a product idea, a concept into the market, to see if you can get it funded by people, like commit to buy it before you even develop it. That is a new kind of model. You build these communities of people that really have a need [and] they work with you to develop the need. They agree that you are the right provider of that need, and then you have an immediate sale. That way, you create lower-cost prototypes right away and you get them to the marketplace quickly."

## THE BUSINESS POWER OF PURPOSE

When you decided to open your business, you probably had a purpose—probably a personal one. Studies have shown that entrepreneurs are usually motivated by freedom and creativity. The idea of being your own boss, making your own money, and setting your own hours is appealing to many of us, but that may not be how it is turning out.

Mitch Russo is the author of *The Invisible Organization: How Ingenious CEOs Are Creating Thriving Virtual Companies*. His book explains how to double or even triple any business quickly without increasing overhead—and in most cases, decreasing it. Mitch is also behind Business Breakthroughs International, a company once owned by Tony Robbins and Chet Holmes. He joked with me, "It was great when I started working for myself! I suddenly was able to work only part-time . . . 12 hours a day."

If you can relate to that because you're working way more hours for less money and more stress than you ever thought you would, here's the good news: by increasing the number of qualified prospects who flow toward you, and treating them well, you will increase your revenues, which makes running and growing your business easier.

# Chapter 6

# The Peculiar Principle of "Givers Gain"

In his landmark, life-changing book, *Influence: The Psychology of Persuasion*, Robert B. Cialdini introduces principles his research proves will trigger subconscious, even primal, reactions in other human beings. These are reactions that include motivating people to buy from you.

One especially valuable rule that Cialdini defined is the "Rule of Reciprocity." That is: When you give someone something, they feel an obligation to give you something in exchange. We all have a similar unconscious behavior, and it is true in every culture in the world.

"We are here because our ancestors learned to share their food and their skills in an honored network of obligation." (*Influence*, 2009, p. 19) The early modern human hunter-gatherers traded furs for fish; the blacksmith mended the horse's shoe in return for a plump chicken or two; today, you trade your dollars for some farmer's produce or some manufacturer's piece of plastic.

In some cultures, the whole system is greased by valuable gifts and exchanges of money. Well-mannered people in the civilized world would never show up at a dinner party without bringing a little something for the host. Many offices have a bowl of candy on the receptionist's desk.

The Rule of Reciprocity works in business. You've been the unwitting target of businesses using this rule all your life. The vineyard offers you a sampling of their finest wines. Will you really leave the tasting without buying a bottle? What action do you feel inclined to take when going past that cookie shop in the mall or near the fragrance boutique when they give you a morsel or a whiff? This "free sample" is meant to trigger the reciprocation instinct in you, whether the purveyor is actively conscious of the fact or not.

There's a more succinct way to explain this rule. Ernestine Fischer, a self-help guru, simply stated it as "Givers Gain."

When you give something to others, you gain something in return.

You may be giving to make others feel better, to make them take a specific action, to go on a date with you, or to hand you their credit card. In each case, you are giving something with the hope of gaining something in return. I suspect that Ernestine meant to give selflessly, with no thought of return, but that takes some super human effort. Even when we donate to charity, we are secretly expecting that warm, fuzzy feeling we'll get inside. In your business, you can enact this rule easily by giving stuff away. In fact, the more you give away, the more customers you will attract.

Could you implement any of these?

- Give a month free when a customer buys your service today.
- Give away extra coffee filters or a bag of premium roast beans with every coffee machine you sell.
- Hand out your food item on the aisle corners at Costco or another grocery store.
- Write a book and then give people access to an informative free video or two on the subject, or classes, courses or webinars. (Go to www.KellerMedia.com/webinars for free downloads, videos, and more.)
- Offer a free download of a track from your newest music CD.
- Give away a water bottle with your company name on it when a customer signs up at your gym.
- Give a free 30-minute consultation before someone hires your therapeutic or financial services.
- Write an ebook about the things people need to know before they hire someone or buy something, like a carpet cleaner.

The "try it before you buy it" is what the consumers sees on the surface. The effect of the Rule of Reciprocity is how the business owner benefits. What can you give away that has a high perceived value in the eyes of your prospects?

## WHAT TO GIVE AWAY

Other than samples or extended service, here are some other items you can give completely free:

- Audio downloads
- Physical books
- Worksheets
- 10-step guides (white papers)
- Webinars
- Seminars or workshops
- Instruction guides
- Training videos
- Top ten lists
- Infographics (as PDFs or inserts)
- ebooks

The "how" to creating most of that stuff is in future chapters of this book.

The best thing to give away is something that will not cost you shipping or handling time. When you digitally deliver a free item, you create it once and can deliver it automatically forever.

When you give something away online, you usually trade their first name (at the least) and email address for the free giveaway. This way you get to build your mailing list and with their permission, you can send them future mailings, promotions, and emails. The freemium is the first step in the relationship.

Giving is a foundation stone in a strong platform. As you build your platform, notice what other businesses around you are offering. You will get all kinds of ideas.

## OF FREEMIUMS AND PREMIUMS

Things you give away to bring in more business are called a "freemium" (a "free + premium") or a "premium." A "freemium" is marketing jargon for something valuable that you give away to people to encourage them to take a specific, usually small, action. This action might be signing up for your newsletter, coming into your store to collect the freemium, listening to a sales presentation (like a time-share pitch), giving away an ebook, or watching a video. You want to provide a freemium that has the highest possible perceived value to your customer but that costs you little or nothing. A freemium is also sometimes called a "lead magnet" because it positively attracts clients to you.

A "premium" is meant to incentivize someone to purchase. A premium is something extra you get when you buy "today" or buy "in the next 15 minutes and we'll DOUBLE your order!"

But wait, there's more!

When I was a 15-year-old telemarketer calling people's houses during the dinner hour, trying to sell them a restaurant coupon book, the premium we offered was a watch. We made a big deal out of these watches. We talked about the "quartz movement" and asked if they wanted it in the gold or the silver tone.

It turned out the watches were junk. The few that worked fell apart within days of receipt. Oddly, the coupon books were legitimate and that was what the customers had actually bought, but the sky-high returns we got on the coupon books were mostly because the watches were so crummy.

I learned a good lesson about freemiums and premiums from that experience, and I'm passing it along to you: make sure that whatever you give them is of high quality, even if it is "just" information. You probably know more about the subject of your expertise than 90 percent of your customers. This makes your information high quality. Take the time to prepare and deliver it nicely.

The Rule of Reciprocity can start transforming your business right away. Now, at the end of every blog post, offer a copy of your free ebook or video or audio download.

# Chapter 7

# Content Creation Strategies

Smart content creation is a way of choosing what material has the best chance of getting into the minds of your prospects and that provides enough value to make them want to take the next step with you.

Whatever form or format you want to put it in, you will need to have content. Content fills blogs, ebooks, audio programs, marketing campaigns, podcasts, webinars, and workshops. This section is on how to easily create content that you can use for any purpose you desire.

It is a lot of work to come up with enough compelling, interesting, readable content every day to fill a newspaper.

Regular people like you and I now take on the responsibility for creating enormous amounts of content to fill up blogs, websites, social media, and more—all in addition to our day jobs!

How does one person come up with good stuff over and over? Is there a way to make it easier? Yes! Lucky for you, this chapter will help you (or the people to whom you delegate your content creation) understand the core organizing principles of content creation. You will also learn how to generate lots of great ideas in the shortest period of time, to fill in during the times you aren't feeling inspired.

Assuming you are clear on your USP and your customer avatars (you should be by this point in the book!), you will want to make certain you create content that is in alignment with your brand identity, that will build the relationship between you and your audience, encourage people to like you and trust your opinion, and motivate them to take actions you recommend (buying, protesting, enrolling, voting, changing, etc.). There is no point in sharing content that doesn't build your brand and attract more customers to you.

The first guiding principle of content creation is this: You must provide valuable, consistent, organized content. People want the security of getting what they came for when they approach your content. When you consistently deliver that, you become a valuable resource in their lives.

Content can only do these four things:

*When you are young, you look at television and think, there is a conspiracy. The networks have conspired to dumb us down. But when you get a little older, you realize that is not true. The networks are in business to give people exactly what they want.*

—Steve Jobs

1. *Inspire.* Content that inspires is meant to make a person feel good, happier, to think loftier thoughts, and to dream bigger dreams. The story of a hero who overcame amazing odds is an inspiring story.
2. *Entertain.* Entertainment could be a fiction book or a funny kitten video.
3. *Inform.* This is the news—people are not usually going to take action based on it, but they want to know about it. How many kilowatt-hours of energy your town consumed last year is just information (data), nothing more to most people.
4. *Educate.* This is the content that teaches someone how to do something or perhaps how to think about something. A recipe is an education piece. So are the topics "How to Save Money on Your Groceries" and "Choosing the Right Financial Advisor."

When a person consumes your content in any form, they have a goal in mind, even if they are not conscious of it. The explosion of companies creating funny videos and posting them on YouTube is evidence of this.

## ORGANIZING YOUR CONTENT

Your job as a content creator is to find out what people want and give it to them. The better you do that, the faster you will build your platform and the more customers you will attract. That's all there is to it.

An article titled, "Five Ways to Save Money on Your Electric Bill" would be a disappointment if most of it ended up being an anecdote about the writer's trip to Home Depot to buy insulation, or a diatribe about why saving on utilities will help the planet stay green, or if it accidentally only offers three methods when it promised five. Content must be organized and deliver on its promise.

A few years ago while on vacation, I needed some aspirin. I went into what I thought was a tiny drug store in a mid-sized Italian town. To my American way of thinking, this was the strangest retail experience of my life. In one six-inch section of a metal pegboard display, I saw the following items grouped together:

- Ladies' tights
- Baby bottles
- Two types of toothpaste

The toothbrushes and floss were four aisles away from the toothpaste. Cheap costume jewelry was right next to plastic spa shoes and men's underwear. When I checked out with my aspirin, I noticed that the products massed around the cash register (what is called a "Point of Purchase" display) were Ace-style elastic bandages and rubber spatulas. This product jumble made no sense to me at all.

Sometimes, people do this same thing with their content. On a Facebook public page intended to attract more people to their business-consulting services, they suddenly share a video from YouTube about a funny kitten. Or they go off on a tangent and rant about bad drivers, but never tie these extraneous topics into their core message or their USP.

Resist the urge to sell the equivalent of Ace bandages and rubber spatulas at your point-of-purchase display. If you have a passion to talk about two disparate topics, create two disparate brands and do not commingle your audiences. Your audience should not wonder what your purpose is and must not think you are mentally scattered, which comes across as unreliable. People do business with people they like and trust. Your words should always convey that you are reliable, trustworthy, and likeable . . . and that you have the solution they are seeking. Trust is built by giving people what they expect from you, consistently and of high value, as promised.

The next component is that the content must be valuable in alignment with what your audience wants and needs from you and your content.

## HOW TO GATHER GOOD CONTENT

These are three ways to gather content:

1. Generate original content yourself.
2. Become an aggregator of content created by others.

3. Pay others to create content for you.

Whichever method or combination of methods you choose, as the "brain behind the brand," you will need to stay focused on what kind of content fits the image you want the public to have of your company.

## HOW TO BRAINSTORM CONTENT IDEAS

Brainstorming a lot of ideas all at once will allow you to pick and choose what content matches your brand, which to develop, and how to spark new ideas going forward.

The intended outcome of the brainstorming methods below is to help you come up with as many ideas as fast as possible. Some of them will not seem like good ideas tomorrow. Others will. Some will foster even more and better ideas later. You can test them on your audience (review Chapter 3, "Analytics and Espionage"). Your goal is just to get as many ideas as quickly and efficiently as you can. You can sort them out later.

### Ten-Step Group Brainstorming

If you have a few other people who really know your subject matter and care about your success, try group brainstorming. Include every person on your team, from the lowest-paid to the highest, then follow these steps:

1. Set aside 30 to 60 minutes at a time of day when you are at your mental best. (You are the emcee, so choose what works best for you. Your positive energy will have a good effect on the others).
2. Choose a quiet, comfortable place that you find inspiring. Ideally, a place that has a water feature seems to be stimulating for most people, even if it is just a nice framed watercolor of the ocean or a desk fountain. Pick a place where you won't be disturbed. Restaurants are not a good choice because the wait staff seems to always show up at the wrong time.
3. Invite your people.
4. Bring a recording device—the one on your smartphone may work just fine. You want all ideas to be recorded.
5. Provide everyone with a notepad and a pen so each of you can jot things down.
6. Turn off all cell phones (unless you are using one to record), tell others not to disturb you, and then prepare to hunker down. Everyone should have gone to the bathroom, gotten coffee, etc.
7. Set the rules at the beginning. Rule #1—there is no judgment of any idea presented. No scowls, no head shaking, no verbal retorts. Do not stop, scorn, deride

or insult, compliment, encourage, or expound any ideas that come up. The goal is to expand and freely explore new and innovative ideas. Going off the rails will happen and is desirable.

8. Encourage everyone to bring up ideas, as many ideas as they can, in any order, no matter who is speaking. Do not let anyone monopolize the conversation. Since going from person to person might inhibit flow, it is usually advisable to let the eager ones speak first, but then ask each of the quieter people if they have anything to add.

9. When the session is over, send the recording to www.Rev.com (or a comparable transcription website) to get it transcribed quickly.

10. Send a copy of the transcript to all participants. Ask each participant to privately review the transcript and highlight any ideas that still seem like good ones. Ask for feedback or votes.

## Solo Brainstorming

Brainstorming by yourself is easiest if you take the following steps:

1. Choose a time and place where you will not be disturbed or distracted. My personal preference is in whatever hotel room I find myself in when I am on the road speaking. The fact that I am in an unfamiliar yet safe environment seems to trigger my brain to think outside the ruts it has created.

2. Prior to the brainstorming session, do something physical for 5 to 10 minutes that gets you breathing deeply. This could be a brisk walk; some conscious, quick deep breathing; some yoga asanas; or even a dozen jumping jacks. Oxygen empowers your brain.

3. Sit down with a recording device (and a notepad and pen if that is your style). Set a timer for 30 minutes.

4. Solemnly commit to creating the best content ideas you can in the time allotted; ones that grow your business, build your brand, and serve your public at the highest level possible.

5. Begin! Speak and/or write as many ideas you can, without self-criticism or judgment, as they pour out of your brain. If the word "orthodontist" slips off your tongue while you're brainstorming and you remember you need to make an appointment for your teen, just keep on going. Everything is being recorded. Ignore your inner critic. Let your brain be a volcano of ideas, each one tossed up into the air. You can sort and develop the good ones later.

6. When the timer dings, quickly decide if you are on a roll and whether or not you want to keep going.

7. If you have recorded your ideas aloud, get them transcribed and highlight the ones you like best. Develop and implement the ones that have the most promise.

Try brainstorming with your customers, your friends, your mastermind group, your romantic partner, or your teenager. You will be surprised how differently people think about the exact same subject. Remember not to immediately reject any idea and to allow every single idea, however crazy it sounds at first. When you have completed these exercises, you will have a sizable list of ideas, and many of them will be good ones!

## HOW TO KNOW IF YOUR CONTENT IS GOOD

But how will you know if your content is any good? How do you know which ideas to develop? In a lifetime of content creation, I've deduced there are two ways: what comes together naturally and what elicits the intended response from the intended audience.

"Comes together naturally" means the idea you created for the article, the blog, the script for the web video, or whatever it is—fits together. You can easily help the reader move from point A to point B in a logical flow. The reader should get value from the time they invest in consuming your content in any form or format.

Remember this: someone engaging with your content is investing their energy—a limited supply—in your message. Grow your business by giving them what they want. How do you know what content will elicit the best response from your audience? In the beginning, you cannot know until you put it out there.

I work with many authors and speakers who are trying to pick the best content concept—the one that is going to fly with their audience and sell the most books or get them the highest fees for their speeches. Here's a technique you can modify for your own benefit.

Take the general theme, the point, the goal of your content. Sketch out six ways you can split it into sub-points, steps, or details. Break each of those into two parts and write content and/or create video content on each of them. Using your social media platform (see Chapter 10), execute a test on each of the 12 pieces. Post each at the same time of day on a Tuesday, Wednesday or Thursday. Do what is called "boosting a post" on Facebook. On any public page, they will allow you to put just a little money on any post and they will promote it to a set number of people. (Choose your avatars! To find out more, read Perry Marshall's *Ultimate Guide to Facebook Marketing*.) It will take only a few minutes to learn how to boost a post. So put a little ad money ($10 to $20) behind each of the 12 and then watch what people respond to best. Take the one or two best ideas and replicate a marketing test on social media using just those ideas with the same budget. Is there a clear winner when you've run 1,000 people past both of them? That's what the world wants from you.

If you see that one gets 15 responses and the others only get one or two, create another piece of content similar to the one that got the 15 responses and see if it was a fluke or if it happens again. (See Chapter 3 on Analytics.) The world will point you to the direction it wants you to go. People vote with their comments (even the nasty ones!) and with their like buttons.

So how do you know if your content has achieved your goal? By the response you get. Are more people coming toward you? Are they buying, engaging, and interacting how you want? If not, what are your options? When you give people lots of good stuff (stuff they want) you become their preferred provider and they become your fans, your customers, and your followers.

Give the people more of exactly what they want. Be like Steve Jobs.

## THE VALUE OF AN EDITORIAL CALENDAR

The media manages content development via what is called an "editorial calendar." This technique is very helpful for you to use, too. It is wise to develop one for yourself to organize the content of your blogs, ebooks, videos, or any other content you want to create. This will save you work, reduce redundancy, make it easier for you and any support team you have to follow and help you pre-plan for special events.

For example, a magazine's editorial calendar will be planned out at least a year in advance. It might say that the focus for the April edition will be "Decorating for Spring" and "Simple Spring Cleaning Tips." The editors know in advance that the July edition will have an article on "How to Host a Terrific Independence Day Celebration" and feature recipes and decorations readers can make themselves.

Although it is less evident and more subject to change, a newspaper's editorial calendar is similar. They know that section one will be all about politics, and whatever is going on at the moment locally or nationally; section two will contain features about local people, bands, and events; section four is about sports, and so on.

How can this help you? By creating a large amount of content ideas all at once, like you did while brainstorming. Now think of them as puzzle pieces and putting them in the frame (the editorial calendar) so you can complete a picture that makes sense for your business goals. If you are going to be offering a special Christmas sale to push people into buying your product at the end of the year, you will want to start prepping your audience in early November at the latest. With an editorial calendar, you can see at a glance the subject of the content you want to release in March, and the places you can repurpose content already created. If your business is seasonal, you want to create articles and blogs and media pitches (see Chapters 17 to 19 on getting media) that match your seasonal flow.

A specified monthly theme gives you clarity on what you and your team need to create and when. It also gives you ideas for how to shade your content according to what the majority of your audience is thinking about now.

## HOW TO ASSEMBLE AN EDITORIAL CALENDAR

1. Get 12 sheets of blank copier paper and label each with the name of a month.
2. Mark the major holidays in your country on each month (e.g., Hanukah and Christmas).
3. Use the brainstorming techniques below to come up with every idea you can about how you could create content for each month, each season, each holiday, or any other reason you can think up.
4. Transfer your completed plan to a wall calendar.

Next, I recommend you go to your favorite office supply store and buy a huge wall calendar. Fill in the boxes with your master editorial calendar so you and anyone else who helps you create your content, can see it at a glance. Got a spare 15 minutes? Sit down and write a blog post on the next topic due.

Then you can either create the content from a list of your best ideas, find other people's blogs/content on topics you have selected, or hire someone to write for you.

*Hint*: The easiest way to fill the calendar is to brainstorm a massive number of ideas—so many that you have ideas to spare.

This method will give you plenty of content to give away, so you become more likable and trustable, and gain a reputation as a creator of quality content.

# Chapter 8

# The Content Creation Dilemma: How to Avoid Procrastination

In publishing, we know that people who buy one diet book will buy 15. People who are broke will buy a dozen books on fixing their credit or making money fast. We joke around and call the whole category, "Shelf Help" because judging by results, the only thing being helped by these purchases is the shelf on which they sit so pretty.

Decades ago, I noticed that most people never open any kind of information product they buy. Many multi-level marketers have closets full of the product they sell, unopened. Publishing industry research indicates that most people allegedly never read past the third chapter of a book, no matter how much they want the desired result. (Give yourself a BIG hug if you just read this paragraph—you're one of the winners!)

Years ago at a business luncheon, I was seated beside an infomercial celebrity. He told me that his money-making system had transformed many thousands of lives. I said it had not, because people don't open the product (much less take action) on most of the stuff they buy, no matter how much they believe it would be good for them to do so. That's just human nature.

He said he didn't believe me, but something must have stuck in his mind. Less than a year later, he called me to tell me I was right. His product was sold as a lot of paper with six audio cassettes pressed into a specially molded front cover of a binder, and then all of it shrink-wrapped closed. As an experiment, his marketing company sent out 60 of their products without the cassette tapes inside, just the paper. Anyone taking off the shrink-wrap would have instantly noticed that they were missing. Out of the 60 they sent out without the cassettes, only one customer ever called to complain . . . and that was six months after the experiment!

While this is bad news for the entire human race, it is great news for us platform builders. It means that all the drama in your head and all the good reasons that are holding you back from creating something are preposterous.

You don't need to wait until you can afford a camera crew to start making your promotional videos. You don't need to wait until you find the perfect recording studio to start putting out a podcast. You don't need to wait until you can afford to hire a writer before you start blogging. Just get going! The fact is, there is nothing stopping you from building your platform right now.

The obvious conclusion: It's better to do a good enough job than to do nothing while you wait for perfect. You will never get the results you want from the actions you do not take.

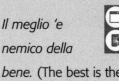

*Il meglio 'e nemico della bene.* (The best is the enemy of the good [enough].)

—16th-century Italian proverb

# Chapter 9

# How to Write and Sell an eBook

An ebook is an excellent choice for a freemium, a premium, or even as a product itself. It allows you to give valuable knowledge to people, which anchors your expertise in their minds. It also entitles you to tactfully pitch them while they are reading. Best of all, an ebook is the easiest way to attract the benefits from the principle of "Givers Gain."

The benefit of having one or more ebooks is that you can trade this freemium in exchange for at least the first name and email address of your potential customers.

Before you think, "I can't write!" or "I don't want to write a whole book just to give it away!" let me assure you that an ebook is a great giveaway, worth the effort, and doesn't have to be anywhere near as long as a "regular" book.

For example, the book you are reading is about 64,000 words long, but there's no rule that says you have to write something this long to give away. You can write an ebook on one specific topic that satisfies and delights people with just 15 to 20 pages. In fact, I've had some clients use one-page "Top Ten" lists or guides or even infographics as giveaways, and they work.

I'm going to give you the easiest, fastest ways to get an ebook done in four steps.

## STEP ONE: DECIDE ON YOUR CONTENT

It will be a lot easier when you know what you want to write about!

Toy with these ideas:

- The Top 10 Worst Mistakes People Make When [acquiring your product or service] and How You Can Avoid Them
- Five Ways to Make Sure YOU (Always/Never) Get _____ Again!
- What Every _____ Needs to Know About _____

Are you coming up with some ideas?

If those didn't trigger something easy—something you could rattle off the top of your head—ask yourself these questions:

- What do my customers tell me they find most daunting when they want to purchase a product or service like mine?
- What is the most common complaint I hear from customers about my competitors?
- What do customers like most about having purchased the product? Are they happier, richer, thinner, or healthier?
- How many times a year/lifetime does a typical person need the product or service I sell?

If it is infrequent and/or expensive, e.g., wedding planning, can you strike fear in their hearts with how to make sure they do it right? If it is "too" frequent (from their perspective) can you explain to them why they want to look for higher quality/better maintenance/how to extend the useful life of the product or service you sell?

For example, you sell air conditioning units and people need someone to change their filter because it will extend the life of their system. An estimated 1,800 microbes are in the air we breathe—one Panasonic air conditioner claims to get rid of 99 percent of them! Help your customer think about all the time they'll save by not dusting and not breathing in who-knows-what. If they have a baby or an elderly person living with them, or suffer from asthma, point out that 99 percent of all microbes will be gone! Or write an ebook about pollution inside the home.

What is the number one most unusual or surprising thing about the way your industry/business works—something people who just start working in it are always surprised to see?

My public relations professor at Arizona State University told our class a story that has always stuck with me. It has informed many marketing decisions I have made for my own company and helped me consult with many clients. The story was about the then-independent Coors Brewing Company. Coors now operates the seventh largest brewery in the world in Golden, Colorado.

Apparently, long ago, the attempt to gain market share against Pabst or Budweiser was not going too well, so they hired a new marketing company. The new marketing team came in for a tour of the brewery. The team was stunned when they saw the elaborate, meticulous purification process that the water goes through before it is turned into beer.

The marketing team proposed to focus on the incredible purity of the water as the heart of the new ad campaign they were preparing. The Coors executives said, "But everybody who makes beer uses a similar process." The magic words that the marketing people said before they launched one of the most successful marketing campaigns ever up to that point in history: "Yes, but everybody doesn't know that."

The purification process was ho-hum to the brewers, but fascinating and reassuring to the public. Sales skyrocketed. And any Johnny-come-lately companies who might have said, "But, wait! We use the same system" would have looked disgruntled or like also-rans.

What ideas for content can you draw from that story? Are there systems or processes in your business, either ones you built because you wanted to do it better, or industry standards that could be the differentiation your company needs to attract more customers?

One ebook about any of these is terrific, but eventually writing ebooks on all of them will give you the chance to swap them out and test which one pulls in the most new business.

## Make an Outline

Now that you have your first ebook concept in mind, take an hour to sketch out the basic sub-themes. What points will prove your ebook's promised result? Three to five should be plenty. Remember, by educating the consumer, you are helping them like and trust you—and buy from you.

Here's an example of an imaginary ebook outline for a speaker or business consultant who wants to capture a niche in the appliance sales industry.

*Tentative Title*:

Why Most Appliance Sales Professionals Quit in the First Year—and
How You Can Succeed

*Outline*:

1. High salesperson turnover happens because most people don't know how to sell; or they think selling appliances is an interim profession until they get a

"real" job; or the business is family run and there is no room to move up; or they believe the store does not bring in enough customers to make a living from straight commissions. Tell the story of Jane Doe, who got fired from a job making $45,000 and begrudgingly became an appliance sales person—and in her first year, earned $117,540 using the methods you teach to your private consulting clients.

2. The importance of attitude—Jane's attitude made all the difference. Once she started seeing how many people quit in Year One, she realized she could earn "old timer" status in a matter of months. That meant that the owner would want her to handle the most important customers.

3. "Show me the money." In this section, you can talk about the difference between selling one-offs—just a washer-dryer set to one residential customer at a time—and selling appliances to owner/operators of multi-family buildings, apartments, condos, etc. Talk about how your coaching client, downsized 61-year-old Frank Bushwhacker, a former engineer, who had never been in a sales role before in his life, used the sales system you share only with your consulting clients to help him attract corporate clients.

Obviously, this is a fictional idea. Appliances are one of the only things I have never sold in my life! If this was your expertise, however, and you wanted to sell yourself as a speaker, coach, or consultant to appliance sales people or their managers, then this would be a great way to tempt appliance sales people into hiring you. Or you could simultaneously be selling yourself directly to all different kinds of sales people, just by changing the examples you use and some of the jargon.

An ebook will work with any type of service you provide and many products.

For a product example, let's say you sell candle-making equipment to amateurs. Your ebook could be all about how to choose the right kind of wax based on scent throw and melt time, and how to choose the right size wick based on candle diameter. Yes, this information is all over the internet for free, which is why the fact that you have taken the time to assemble it in an ebook format, heavily branded with your name, logo, website, and maybe a 10 percent off discount to your online store, will move you to the head of the class.

## STEP TWO: THE EASIEST WAYS TO WRITE

Once you know what you want to talk about and have roughed out an outline from which you can wax lyrical (pun intended if you're the one selling to candle-making hobbyists), you are ready to fill the ebook with valuable, organized content. Here are two methods that work equally well.

## Dictation Method

If you are a better speaker than typist, and you would like to make this process easy on yourself, all you have to do is sketch out your outline. Then, using your smartphone or your computer's sound recorder, record yourself talking about the topic. The average person speaks 110 to 150 words per minute. There are between 4,125 and 5,500 words on average in a 15- to 20-page book. So can you spare 37 to 49 minutes? That seems like very little time to create an ebook, doesn't it? Do not stress over trying to organize it perfectly, just talk naturally. Edit it later or have someone else do that part.

When the audio file is complete, look up www.Rev.com. Sign up, send them your file, and let them transcribe it for you. You can edit it when it gets back.

Voila! Your ebook is nearly done.

## Typing Method

If you think while you type, like I do, I recommend setting aside just two to three hours on a day when you are relaxed, and you can focus on this task. Take your outline and write to match it, so you are sure you cover every topic you intended. Now don't look at the document for three days, so the words fade from your short-term memory. Go back over it just once with a red pen. Ta-daa! Make the changes, and you've finished your ebook!

See how easy that was?

Either way, make sure you include several success stories from people who worked with you or consumed your product or service. Mention that a few years back, John Smith came to you and had X problem, but after working with you for X months (or using your product), poof! His problem was solved. Use good examples. The general reason most customers come to you is to get a solution to a problem, improve their lives in some way. For example, they have roaches in their kitchen, they cannot lose weight, they have the infernal back pain. Talk about your client's relief, joy, success, or health after he encountered your phenomenal work.

If you do not have a signed release from your customer, patient, or client whom you wish to use as an example, create a montage of a typical customer and the result they get when they work with you. Without a release, always make sure you change identifying details like age, name, gender, location, etc. so that the original person cannot recognize him or herself in the story. (You really do not want to be sued for libel, do you?)

You have earned the right to pitch your goods simply because you gave them a solution for free. Subtly pitch throughout the document and dedicate the whole last page to pitching. Put your contact information boldly on the back page. Invite them to go to a hyperlink where you are giving something else away, or where they can watch a

## DON'T WANT TO WRITE A WORD? CAN'T WRITE? DON'T HAVE TIME?

There are plenty of qualified writers in the world who would be happy to have work writing your ebook. Most will ask to record an interview with you once or twice so they can get clear about what you want to say. Then they will write the first draft and send it back to you for review and suggestions.

You can find writers all over the place. Normal payment terms are a small amount down (25 to 50 percent of the total cost of the job) and then the balance is due when you're satisfied. Look for writers who have produced similar content. Some places to find them? Try www.eLance.com, www.ODesk.com or www.LinkedIn.com as a start.

short video of you talking more about the topic. Offer them a discount code because they read the ebook. Offer another surprise bonus, anything special or something that invites them to take one more baby step closer to your cash register.

Read your whole ebook over one more time—aloud. It is amazing how things read different when you hear them aloud.

### How to Edit

You may want to get your ebook professionally edited. Even professional writers need editors. Michelle Martinez, one of the women who edited this book, found all kinds of errors and omissions in this book, and I'm a professional writer. Everyone needs an editor!

You can use your own child who is getting As in high school English; your employee with a good grasp of the English language and a good writer; or hire a college student or junior college adjunct English professor by placing an ad on the community college job board or at www.Cragislist.org. Editing an ebook up to 20 pages can range from $40 to $100. You want to assign your editor three tasks:

1. Does the content make sense to someone with no knowledge of the subject? If not, where does it not make sense?
2. Is the English in proper form? Grammar, spelling, and punctuation.
3. Does it read well? Often, we are so excited about some facet it is easy to go off on a tangent. It may fascinate us, but someone else may fall asleep during the first page. Ask for truth.

Once the contents are completed, it is time to go on to the physical structure of your ebook, and then how to start benefitting from your creation.

## STEP THREE: STRUCTURE, FORMAT, AND DELIVERY METHODS

Here are the basics on structuring and formatting an ebook using Microsoft Word, the most common word processing program used by businesses.

If you think people will print out your ebook in order to read it, use a serif font to increase readability. I recommend 12- or 14-point type for the body, 16 point for the subheadings, 22 point bold for the chapter headings, if any. (A serif font is one in which the lower case letter "h" has little feet. For example, look up Times New Roman "hhhh" in a word-processing program.)

If your ebook is short (ten or fewer pages) and people are likely to read it online or on an ereader, I suggest you use Verdana or any other easily read "sans" (without) serif font you prefer. (No little feet on the letter "h.") I recommend 10- or 12-point type, 16 point for the subheadings, and 22 point bold for the chapter headings, if any.

Give every page a one-inch margin all around the edges and double space the entire document so it reads more easily. Make sure to put a page number on every page, except the first one. Put your contact information (URL, address and phone number), and if you choose, the © copyright information. You may want to add a table of contents if it is more than ten pages long.

Decide if you will add images. Images make it more interesting and sometimes, a picture is worth a thousand words. *Warning*: In principle, you should purchase the license for any images you use. Go to www.GettyImages.com, www.ShutterStock.com, or www.DreamsTime.com to acquire them. Remember what Jeff Hayzlett said earlier about thinking big and what Ford Saeks said about the important of first impressions? Yeah, go big or go home.

Next, create a terrific cover page. It can be elaborate, an image, or professionally designed. You can go to www.Fiverr.com and get a decent cover designed for just $5. Or you can just type the title of the ebook in a big, bold font. Include your name and contact information. Paste the cover art to the top of the document.

Now turn the whole thing into an ebook. This is so easy! Save the finished Word document, and then save it again by selecting "Save As" and then choosing ".PDF" from the drop down list. (This only works if you have a version of Adobe installed. It is free as of this writing.)

You will now have two versions—the Word document in case you want to change something in the future; and the PDF you will share with prospects. One added benefit of delivering it in a PDF format is that it is very difficult for someone to modify your words. That means any unethical competitor won't be able to rebrand it and claim it as theirs and no one will be able to go in and easily change the copy in a way that you may not approve.

To ensure your copyright is protected, you may want to register your ebook with the U.S. copyright office. Form TX will help you do that and provide full instructions. (Find out more at www.copyright.gov/forms/formtx.pdf).

All that remains is setting up a way for your PDF ebook to be automatically delivered to your customer in return for—at the very least—their first name and email address. If you have a web expert on your team, ask for their suggestions. Otherwise, take a look at these auto-responder providers:

- www.MailChimp.com
- www.Infusionsoft.com (this is what we use at Keller Media)
- www.ConstantContact.com

An "auto-responder" is a piece of software that will automatically send a pre-determined email on your behalf to anyone who takes a certain action, such as filling out a form on your website to request your ebook.

Now all you have to do is start offering your ebook at the bottom of your blogs, on Facebook, on your business cards, on your website, on a sign in your store, at parties, with complementary business owners who may have mailing lists that might like your ebook as a bonus to their own people, and so on. You may want to promote it by running Google or Facebook ads (recommended reading: Perry Marshall's *Ultimate Guide to Google AdWords* and *Ultimate Guide to Facebook Advertising*). Your entire platform strategy could be focused just on inducing people to take your high quality, good looking, immediately delivered free ebooks.

Done right, your ebook will make such a positive first impression that it will encourage customers to like and trust you enough to do business with you.

## STEP FOUR: HOW TO SELL AN eBOOK

There are many direct ways to profit from an ebook. You can sell it, whether directly to customers off your website, in the back of the room when you give a speech, or you can even post it up on Amazon and sell it for $1.99 or so, just to winnow out the people who are just thinking about buying from those who are now ready to put some cash behind the solution you promise.

Technically, the "e" in ebook refers to electronic delivery. The minute you make it a physical book, it becomes something else. Common terms for an ebook that has become physical are "guide" or "special report," or "white paper."

If you want to sell your ebook in physical form anywhere but at live events, you'll want to set up a vendor account with Amazon. There are ample instructions on their site and an excellent tutorial. You will need to set up an ISBN (International System of Book Numbering) for it. That's how a book gets a bar code.

If you want to physically sell your special report, you need to have it printed and bound. I have found the most expedient way of doing this is to put the two files—the graphic cover image and the document itself—on a thumb drive and take it to the FedEx or UPS shipping center, and let them do it for me. That way, I can pay for exactly as many copies as I need, and repeat the process any time I sell out. I do not like inventory because if I decide to update or change something, I want to easily get the newest version ready for distribution.

I have sold ebooks at live events for $10 to $200. In the 1990s, my good friend, the late marketer Ken Kerr, one of the original Disney Imagineers and the guy who Walt Disney turned to for help marketing the Epcot Center, sold content in three-ring binders for $250 each. It was just basically a very long ebook. Ken photocopied it only when a customer ordered it and bought the ring binders at the office supply store down the street from his house. Would a more modern version of Ken's idea work for you?

As with everything, test, test, test. Do you get more prospects when it is free? When it is $10? When it is $3.99? The fact is, once it is done there are many ways you can use your ebook to attract more business.

And 90 to 120 days later, write your next one.

# Chapter 10

# Social Media

There is a dizzying array of social media sites swirling around us right now, and new ones are being created every day, it seems. You could go crazy trying to build your company's presence on all of them! Even if you use a cross-platform promotion tool like BuzzFeed, Hootsuite or Marketo, you can still end up running yourself—or your team—around ragged.

Here are a few of the popular social media sharing sites right now. Probably by the time this book is printed, there will be even more!

- Facebook.com
- Google+
- Instagram.com
- LinkedIn.com
- Periscope.com
- Snapchat.com
- YouTube.com

Want the easiest way to figure out which few will bring you the biggest ROI? Simple.

Avatars and Analytics

Research where your avatars are spending their social media energy. Run a short-term (three months will suffice) foray into the one or two you've chosen. Check your analytics results. Make a decision—are your avatars here?

Once you have made your decision, learn or delegate to a team member how to excel in your chosen environments.

To achieve excellence in any of these particular venues, Entrepreneur Press offers some comprehensive books in their Ultimate Guide Series:

- *LinkedIn for Business*
- *YouTube for Business*
- *Pinterest for Business*
- *Facebook Advertising*
- *Twitter for Business*

As long as you find the ones in which your avatars are most active, you can easily master the strategies for reaching them.

At this time in history, the most comprehensive, inclusive social media platform is Facebook, so the rest of this chapter will be primarily dedicated to how to use it to help you achieve your goals—and why and how it will help you.

## THE SECRET WEAPON: SOCIAL MEDIA

There are so many social media sites you can invest your time in! The big ones are Facebook, LinkedIn, Twitter, Pinterest, places like that. I'll explain some basics to use with any social media site in a few pages, but first I want to talk to you about what the fact we entrepreneurs even have access to social media really means for our success.

When a big company like Procter and Gamble, Johnson and Johnson, or Kellogg wants to introduce a new product to the market, they conduct extensive market research. They hire someone to assemble and interview a group of potential average consumers (avatars). They want to know:

- Do they prefer a pill in a purple coating or a pink one?
- Do they feel more attracted to the box with flowers or the box with the sunburst?
- How do they like the taste of the new cereal? Does it contain enough cinnamon?
- What should the new product's name be?

And questions like that.

Companies much bigger than yours use teams of people to conduct these focus groups. They want to find out if customers are more active on their website between

10 A.M. and noon, or if they click the red or the blue Buy button more often, or if they buy more when the background image features white people in their 20s or 30s or when there is more diversity. There are thousands of components that go into comprehensive analytics and countless hours. In fact, marketers can test 24/7 all sorts of different factors.

One well-known American small household appliance company, whom I tangentially worked with, spent $300,000 testing the color of the apron worn by the woman who promoted their product wore in the infomercial! (Believe it or not, the difference between the number of people who bought the winning color was about 30 percent higher than the two runners-up!)

As small business owners, we don't have time to test all that stuff; it doesn't interest some of us; and it is prodigiously expensive and time-consuming . . . unless . . .

Unless you're willing to do the cheaper, faster, not-as-thorough-but-good-enough method you have available to you for almost nothing. Right now. At your fingertips.

It has never been easier to reach massive numbers of customers, give them what they want and in the way they want it than right now, in your lifetime. The internet allows even the tiniest business to accurately and consistently determine what the customer really wants and how they most want to consume it.

By strategically testing the critical marketing components of your business, your message, your product packaging, etc., you can increase your sales in a consistent manner.

Marketers call it split testing, also known as A/B testing. Split testing asks, "Does the consumer like (product, color, sentence, promise, question, flavor) A more than B?"

The easiest way to do this for yourself is with a Facebook public figure page. (More about that in a moment.) You may already have a Facebook page where you share photos of your pets or loved ones; where you reunited with that person you knew in high school; and now keep in touch with the lives of people who you haven't seen in person for a decade.

We're not talking about that kind of Facebook presence.

A "public figure" page is a public page. Most businesses have them, as do celebrities, speakers, authors, and so forth. If you don't know what I'm talking about, go to Facebook and type in your favorite author's name, the maker of your automobile, or any chain store at which you shop.

## HOW TO CREATE A FACEBOOK PUBLIC FIGURE PAGE

If you don't have one yet for yourself or your business (depending on what brand you're trying to make famous), set up a Facebook public figure page right now, following the instructions below. You'll be glad you did.

### Before You Begin: Create a Banner

A "banner" is the picture image at the top of the page that attracts and welcomes people to your page. Think about the feeling you want people to have when they come to your page—inspired? Impressed with your credentials? Browse around Facebook and look for people who have sites serving the same public as you, and who have at least 3,000 likes on their page. What style are they using for their banners? Usually a banner is a combination of an image, a logo if you have one, your name, if relevant, and a few sentences or statements. Hire a few different people on the website www.Fiverr.com and instruct them in what you want. Four people to try out will cost you only $20! A banner is 851 x 315 pixels.

Check out our agency's banner: www.facebook.com/KellerMediaInc.

My public figure page banner: www.facebook.com/WendyKellerCompassionPage.

A few clients' banners as examples: www.facebook.com/positiveoutlooks, www.facebook.com/Jeffrey.Hayzlett, www.facebook.com/wallacejnichols.

### Create Your Page

Think about the kind of following you wish to attract and then choose whether "Public Figure" or "Community" or any other type of public page might be right for your future. Here are the steps:

1. Go to Facebook.com.
2. Log into your account, using your previously set up username and password.*
3. Click the downward facing triangle icon on the top right.
4. Select "Create Page."
5. Select the appropriate category (i.e., "Public Figure").
6. Choose a category from the drop down provided (i.e., "Author").
7. Enter your professional name, business name or stage name in the field below the drop down (i.e., "Jane Smith").
8. Click "Get Started."
9. Fill out the following fields:
   a. A description of yourself (i.e., "Jane Smith is a *New York Times* bestselling author, inspiring audiences across the world with her paranormal self-help books").
   b. Add your previously created website (www.janesmith.com).
   c. Confirm your new Facebook URL (i.e., "www.facebook.com/JaneSmith-Author").
10. Click "Save Info."
11. Upload a photograph of yourself (i.e., a professionally-done headshot).

12. Click "Next."

13. Upload the banner image you made.

14. Click "Next."

15. Click "Add to Favorites" to add this page to the left side of your Facebook home page for easy access. (Optional)

16. Click "Next."

17. Select who you think your target audience would be, using the fields provided (i.e., geographic location, age, gender, and interests).

18. Click "Next."

19. Click "Save."

20. You're done!

\* If you have not already set up a Facebook account:

1. Go to Facebook.com

2. Fill out required fields (i.e., name, email, password, birthday, gender).

3. Click "Sign Up."

## HOW TO USE YOUR FACEBOOK PUBLIC FIGURE PAGE AS YOUR MARKETING RESEARCH DEPARTMENT

What information about your customers' real needs, wants, and interests would be most valuable to you? The answer to this question depends on how long you've been in business, what you already know with certainty, whether you are selling a product or service, if you're trying to sell more of something or introduce something new, etc.

For example, I work with authors who are trying to create books that will sell to a lot of readers. I encourage them to think of the core concepts of their books as interchangeable. Which is to say, chapter four and chapter six could be swapped if that meant the book would sell better. Sometimes, I observe that a book would attract more publishers (and eventually readers) if the main focus of the book is the current content stuffed in chapter eight, and then the rest of the material was wrapped around that superior content. This can be ascertained with Facebook public page testing.

If you could conclusively determine that the business logo for your company that your niece created is not going to attract as many customers as one done by www.99Designs.com, would you be willing to adapt? Are you flexible? A Facebook public page can do that for you.

If you found out that green and azure are better colors for your product packaging than pink and cream, would you be willing to use this knowledge to help yourself? You know where to find that answer, too.

There's no one right answer! Some people are flexible and in business to make a profit; others just want things done their way, regardless of the success they may or may not create. Test, test, test.

## HOW TO TEST YOUR CONTENT FOR ITS SELL-APPEAL

"Content" can mean the subject matter of your book, the key benefits you believe your product or service delivers to your customers, the main sales points for why someone should buy from you, the language you use to describe your product or service offering, and more. Follow the three steps below to test your content.

### Step One: Split Your Content Concept into Six Chunks

*Example One*: You are writing a book for people who sell expensive equipment (tractors, cars, hardware to corporations, etc.). Break the sales process into six steps:

1. Finding the prospect
2. Getting the appointment with the prospect
3. Connecting with the prospect during the interview
4. Finding out what the prospect needs and wants most
5. Presenting your equipment's features as a solution
6. Closing the sale

*Example Two*: You own a small insurance firm. You need more customers, and you've got some ideas. They are:

1. Why people need to buy more insurance
2. How not having enough insurance can be devastating
3. Why you are the best firm from which to buy
4. How people make insurance buying decisions
5. The risks to one's family of not buying insurance
6. How easy it is to buy insurance

### Step Two: Build Out the Content Chunks

Create two different blogs for each concept—making the same point or expressing the same principle, but in a different way.

Write 12 distinct blogs, 300-500 words long, on each of the six content concepts. Make sure they do not blur between one concept and another or your test results will be murky.

### Step Three: Test the Blogs Against the Real World by Boosting Your Posts

What is "boosting a post"?

Facebook allows you to boost any posting on your public page. This means you can choose an audience of people to whom you want to show your post for a small amount of money, and if you comply with their rules, they will show your post to hundreds or even thousands more people than would see it normally. They will find audiences of people like the people who already like your page and show it to all of them, too.

#### Tips for Boosting Posts

If your business is something people deal with in their personal time, then promote your blogs after 6 P.M. local time. If it is something sold B2B, promote it during business hours.

Pick a time for your blog promotion strategy. A popular option is 10 A.M. local time on a Tuesday, Wednesday, or Thursday. Most marketers have found that people are too busy on Mondays and too lazy on Fridays to take much action.

Boost your 12 blogs at the rate of three per week, posted to your Facebook public page at the same time each day. For example: 10 A.M. Tuesday, Wednesday, and Thursday, every week for four consecutive weeks. Mix up the content so, using the example above, perhaps the two blogs about finding the prospect come out three weeks apart, one on Tuesday at 10 and one on a Thursday at 10, three weeks later. Watch the responses!

Using Facebook's "Boost this Post" feature, put $20 ($10 is OK if that's all you can afford) on each post. To use the post boost feature, Facebook will invite you to select your target audience.

There are entire books on this topic—again, look at Perry Marshall's *Ultimate Guide to Facebook Advertising* to learn a lot about this. If you don't want to become a Facebook marketing expert, simply read on. This is how you find out which of your six sub-topics are most appealing to your audience.

## CHOOSING A FACEBOOK TARGET GROUP

- Do you sell regionally or nationally?
- What is the age range of most of your customers?
- What do you know they like? (e.g., surfing, knitting, the Lakers)
- Do they belong to any specific groups?
- Do you know their gender?
- Anything else that helps Facebook identify them?

Save this group under a specific name and boost your post to that specific group each day. The more specific you can be in who they are, the more effective your ad spend ($10 or $20 per post) will be, and the more precise your test results will be.

## WARNING: GRAPHIC CONTENT

As your social media ramps up, you'll need to shovel an enormous amount of graphics, from Facebook quote posts to LinkedIn articles to branded Pinterest images, to the internet. Recently, my company has fallen in love with www.Snappa.io. It was built for people like me and my team, people with zero graphic skills and zero spare time.

I tracked down Snappa co-founder and CEO Christopher Gimmer and asked him why good graphics are so important. He said, "With so much content being produced, good graphics have become extremely important. Good graphics will boost the credibility of your content and result in better engagement from your audience."

Groan. Who has time for that?

Christopher told me, "Making sure you have at least one image in your post is extremely important since it leads to double the shares on Facebook and Twitter. In addition, well-designed graphics may also get 121 percent more Facebook shares compared to more poorly designed graphics." Read that last sentence again!

I don't know about you, but the last thing I want to do is learn Photoshop or the principles of good design, and I've had mixed luck hiring freelancers. I don't need a graphics person full time. That's why I think Chris' company www.Snappa.io is the best of a new breed—easy, fast, simple to learn, with a great variety and fairly priced.

Give Snappa, or the slightly more difficult to learn www.Canva.com a shot. For product images, check out https://PlaceIt.net. Sites like these will make graphics so much easier for you.

Always pay attention to your analytics. What gets the most likes, shares, and comments on Facebook and your marketing research will show you where to go with your business.

## HOW TO BECOME A STAR ON SOCIAL MEDIA

I have the great honor of representing a man known as "Dodinsky." The chance that you or someone you know has interacted with him on Facebook is extremely high, since he has an aggregate following of more than six million people worldwide!

Dodinsky's books immediately become *New York Times* bestsellers that positively influence the lives of so many people.

He is the brains behind "four pages." Each page caters to a different market/audience. He said, "Per my observation people do not always have the same 'taste' for certain things. So these pages help me capture people according to their interest. So aside from my own 'Dodinsky' page, we have 'The Book Connections' for book lovers, 'The Humor League' for people who love humor, and 'Positive Outlooks' for people who love inspirational quotes and stories."

Dodinsky started on Facebook in 2010, though he had been a top blogger on Myspace for five years before he made the switch.

I asked him how much time he spends fussing with his enormously successful pages. He said, "We don't have to stay on the computer and 'work' the whole day because Facebook fortunately gives you the ability to schedule your posts. But if I were to give an estimate, a good five hours a day could be spent working on the pages."

You will probably just develop and maintain one page, but how would it benefit you to have astonishing growth like Dodinsky has created? With so much traffic, he's been able to get clear on and stay focused on his avatars. You'll want to use the avatar testing and incorporate what you should have just learned from post boosting to get clear on your plan.

Dodinsky says, "The majority of our following is mainly from the United States, Philippines comes second, followed respectively by India, United Kingdom, Canada, and Australia. Eighty percent of our followers are women. They are professionals, blue-collar workers, and housewives. They are coming from different political and religious persuasions, but when it comes to what inspires or make them happy, they have a lot in common. They know that life will test you and bad things can happen, but they choose to be inspired and believe that things will get better." (How's that for knowing one's avatar?)

Remember what I wrote about people doing business with people they like and trust? Absorb that truth from Dodinsky's own words: "I started writing not because I wanted to become a bestselling author. I started to write because there was a time in my life when I was hurting. Writing down my thoughts helped me heal. That was the beginning, and it evolved into sharing my observations and what I think about life's complexities. When I shared my thoughts with the world, I found out that I was not alone and those who read my writings discover that they are not alone. It is a beautiful thing to know you are sharing this 'road' with a lot of people. It brings you comfort to realize that you too can survive life's troubles just like the others."

There are endless books out there about how to master Google+ or LinkedIn. Dodinsky's world-class success has improved the lives of millions. What could your content do? I asked him how you and I could have a similar impact with our own social media. What is his secret to success?

He said, "Truly love what you are doing. You will no doubt have a few stumbles, but you must learn to see them as learning curves. Persistence has created a lot more successful people than pure luck. Be authentic. Do not [strive to] impress people with what you can do. The big audience will come if you start with you—be your own biggest fan!"

I certainly recommend that you fully use and grow your Facebook public page, although a year from now, there could be some other social media strategy to take its place. Do your market testing, yes, but also do what is in your heart to reach the customers you most want to serve.

# Chapter 11

# Recording Sensational Audio

Ronan Chris Murphy is an audio engineer and CEO of Recording Boot Camp. He works with artists as diverse as rock legend King Crimson and YouTube sensation Tay Zonday. He also works on multimillion-dollar video game projects and was an audio lead for Microsoft. He regularly lectures and consults about audio around the world. Before we met, I had no idea that sound quality was all that important.

A few months after we met, Ronan heard one of my webinars. He told me that it sounded like I was at home frying eggs! I was confused. I had been enthusiastic while I presented, my content was organized, my slides were not too word-dense, and I was delivering something about which I am an undisputed expert: platform building.

I didn't know what to do with his feedback, so I ignored it. I'm too busy to think about sound quality! Besides, aren't people there for the content only? They don't expect me to have a legion of sound engineers like Britney Spears or a Hollywood film, do they? But his comment gnawed at my mind.

I interviewed Ronan for this chapter, as much for your sake as mine. I've been to his expansive, glamorous studio in Santa Monica, California. I've seen his blog that uses words I don't understand about equipment that does stuff I don't understand.

I figured maybe it was time you and I figure out how to create great sound quality for webinars, podcasts, products, and online trainings. I asked him my biggest question: Why does it even matter?

Ronan replied, "Sound is important on two fronts: in the perception of your brand and also in the experience of the listener. More specifically, how well the listener can absorb our content. In the early days, a person would get credit for just putting something up online. But now, people expect online content to be more professional. Otherwise, it gives potential customers the idea, 'This doesn't seem quite legitimate.'"

If you are just starting out and can't spend a fortune, but resonate to the truth behind Ronan's words, this chapter will give you his high-level, expert advice on how any of us can sound more professional, competent, and clearer when we are recording any audio.

## HOW HUMANS HEAR

"People are way more sensitive to sound detail than most people ever realize," Ronan said. "With our eyes closed, we can calculate the location of a sound, the distance the sound source is from us, and the type of physical space we are in. We can listen to that tiny speaker in our cell phone and tell if a loved one we are talking to is having a bad day, even if they do not tell us. We are amazing listeners! At the risk of getting too geeky, when we shoot digital videos, the visuals and sounds are broken up into tiny little samples or frames. They use 24- to 60-snapshots per second to produce the visuals and 48,000 per second to produce the audio. Audio conveys a lot of detail!"

The extraneous noises we hear when we are trying to listen to something are always called "ambient" sounds. Right now, as I write this, I can hear a leaf blower the groundskeeper is using somewhere on the property. I hear a car honking its horn; a jet flying overhead; and the timer on my desk clicking to remind me that I have a conference call in 30 minutes. (I like the sound of the old-fashioned cook's timer ticking when I want to be reminded to stay on task for a certain number of minutes.)

If we were having a conversation right now, I wouldn't consciously listen to any of those noises or focus on the reverberation in the space. Our marvelously adaptive brains can screen out lots of ambient noise and we can direct our focus to the "main event."

Curiously, Ronan said that the brain has a harder time doing this after the sound has been recorded. This is because when it is recorded, all of the multiple sounds with unique locations and levels become a single audio event.

This is why, when my computer's microphone picked up the ambient noises around my office and Ronan heard the replay, it sounded like I was home frying eggs. I keep a little kerosene stove and frying pan on my desk for just this purpose. OK, not really! A person standing in front of me would have been able to focus their attention on my voice and automatically filter out a lot of ambient sound.

The problem with excessive ambient noise and reverberation, especially on a recording, is that our brain has to strain to understand the words. When a brain is straining to pick out a voice, energy is used on that rather than absorbing the content of the speaker.

It is like reading without your eyeglasses. An excessive amount of ambience or reverberation is the audio equivalent of things being out of focus. When the listener gets fatigued, it won't be pleasant anymore, and it will be much more challenging to decipher and absorb the content. This is one of the reasons professional voice-over and books-on-tape readers work in special acoustically treated spaces that reduce ambient noise.

Ronan said, "One of the big causes of bad audio in digital content is the fact that many people will record the audio with the built-in mic on their laptop or digital camera. Most of these built-in mics are omnidirectional (they record sound from all directions). When you are speaking, in addition to picking up your voice and the other noises around you, an omnidirectional mic is picking up your voice reverberating off the back wall, the side wall, the ceiling . . ." Ronan explained. "If you have ever noticed how your voice changes when you walk into a tile bathroom, that's an example of the effect." A "directional" mic will pick up sound from just from one direction.

Additionally, laptop and camera mics often use built-in compression, which is when the device is trying to automatically level out differences between loud and quiet sounds. It may bring up the ambient noise and lower the voice to make the levels more consistent. The net result of this can be that your speaking voice will be reduced and the level of the reverberation of your voice will be increased (along with the leaf blowers, computer fans, etc.).

Ronan suggests that the best options for recording audio are to use a lavalier mic or a directional mic. You clip the lavalier, also called a "lav" or lapel mic, right onto your clothing about four fingers' width away from your mouth.

To solve the fried eggs problem, I bought a Samson Q2U. It cost me about $45 and even I can hear the difference in the sound quality I get now even I can hear the difference in the sound quality I get now. I use it to get excellent sound when I plug it into my video camera so I can record videos, vlogs (video blogs), and other programs. Even if the camera is far away from me, the mic remains close to my voice.

> *Once the sound has been recorded, all the sounds become a single audio event.*
>
> —Ronan Chris Murphy, Music Producer/Engineer

When Ronan does his own webinars and training, he prefers to use a Shure SM57 mounted on a mic stand. That's a directional mic you can hold in your hand or put on a stand. They cost about $100 new. These are also called cardioid, hypercardioid or shotgun mics. A DJ at a station is always on a directional microphone. The audio being recorded for a sitcom or on a film set is almost always on a directional microphone, and so is any public speaker you might see at an event.

To plug it into a laptop, you will need an XLR to USB adapter or other interface, starting at around $50. Ronan said that when you see a president giving a speech in the Rose Garden or anywhere else, he's usually using a Shure SM57.

If you plan to project your voice by using any letters that start with a "B" or a "P," (and it is Pretty Perplexing to Produce a Beautiful Program without these two Perfectly Pleasant consonants) you will want to prevent plosives. Plosives are the little gusts of wind we use to form those sounds. These sounds cause a subtle stress on the microphone that can sound like a low boom in the recording. You've seen those little foam balls that slip over the end of a microphone? They are called "windscreens." It will Probably Behoove you to Purchase one.

Directional microphones do an odd thing when you speak very close to them. They exhibit something called the "proximity effect," which is an unnatural boost of low frequencies in the voice. Many radio DJs and movie trailer voice actors use this trick to make their voice sound more full and powerful.

## RONAN CHRIS MURPHY'S THREE TIPS TO MAKING A GREAT RECORDING

1. Use a good mic and place it at the right distance from your mouth.
2. Choose a comfortable place to record that inspires you, but doesn't have a lot of background noise. Go into your house somewhere and clap. Do you hear a lot of reverberation, the sound bouncing around? That's not ideal.
3. Stay away from plate glass, rooms without carpeting, and high ceilings. If you are serious about creating great content, consider creating a space in your home or office specifically designed for great sound.

You may also have seen the mesh circle that sits in front of some microphones, especially in radio stations or some podcasters. The circle, called a "pop filter" gets rid of pops caused by plosives. These perform basically the same function as the windscreen, but they are often about 6 inches in diameter. If you are planning to read a script or look at a computer screen while you are speaking, it may be difficult or inconvenient to see around the pop filter.

## SHOULD YOU HIRE AN ENGINEER?

Ronan advises that "if you are the kind of creator who likes to get inspiration, do it right now, and throw it up online, then doing everything yourself makes sense. If you're the kind of content creator who wants to actually develop something, maybe a product, that is more meticulously created, especially if you are doing a big audio online course, going back to get rid of the 'Ahs' and the 'Ums' is a lot of work. You're probably going to want to find an audio engineer to help you out since he or she can probably edit much faster than you can. Also an engineer can make it sound even better by doing EQ (equalization) and level adjustments."

Equalization means to adjust for how "bright, or dark, or round" the voice sounds. An engineer can also do level adjustments both manually and with tools like compressors to keep the level of the voice consistent and more intelligible. This determines how enjoyable it is to listen to, and if it sounds clear and pleasing on your listening device—whether it be an MP4 played in your car, on your smartphone, or through your laptop. The sound engineer's goal is to master the audio file so you sound great across all kinds of playback systems.

## HOW TO HIRE AN ENGINEER

There are no widely-accepted formal certifications for sound engineers. The first place to start looking is to ask your friends if they have referrals. You can also find engineers on www.Fiverr.com or www. Craigslist.org or on the jobs board at the local junior

When some voices get more intense and excited, especially female voices, they can have a quality that is really piercing when recorded. Too much high frequency is unpleasant or even painful to listen to and will cause a listener to turn down the volume. A good sound engineer can smooth that out so you can get the excitement but not the shrillness. You don't want people to reach for the volume knob to turn you down just because you're feeling enthusiastic.

college. There are people starting out who will be excited to work for $12 to $15 per hour.

A sound engineer doesn't have to live near you. You can upload your recording to www.Dropbox.com or some other cloud file service and they can download it, edit it, and upload it when complete.

To begin, don't hire someone to do an entire program. Just get someone to help you with a 10- to 25-minute special bonus course and see how it goes. That's between one and three hours of work, according to Ronan. See if you have a good working relationship.

- Do you work well together?
- Do they make the process easy for you?
- Do you sound good?
- Do they keep to their promised deadlines?

When you find a sound engineer whose work you like and whose work ethic you can trust, you can delegate larger projects. Ronan said that it actually takes less time per minute. If it is just you speaking into one mic, the sound engineer just has to figure out the EQ and level adjustments that make your voice sound its best and then let it run. All the work is up front. It's fairly simple to go into the file and smooth out the "umms" and the mistakes after that. "If someone tells you it will take six hours of work to fix up an hour of well recorded audio, they're probably not the right person," Ronan advises.

## FOR THE DO-IT-YOURSELFER

Maybe you just like twiddling with stuff. Maybe you love learning new software programs. Maybe you can't afford to hire a sound engineer just yet. Or maybe you want to have the skill to efficiently and properly edit short audio so you can turn it around and post it online super-fast.

I asked Ronan about that, too. His answer surprised me.

He said, "Choose software that you have access to and that you know your friends or family use, too. The features are not as important as having people on call who can help you out of technical jams while you learn." As you learn any program, you will slam into glitches. Ronan recommends GarageBand for Mac users and Audacity for Windows users.

Now you know why it is important to have the best sound you can and how to get it. It enhances your image and allows your customers to feel confident that you are a professional person, and more importantly, help you better share your content with your customers.

# Chapter 12

# How to Create a Good Audio Product or Program

I believe you should spend a fortune on your website, but as little as possible when you are starting out creating products, freemiums or premiums, especially before you start making a lot more money in your small business.

There are all kinds of audio programs you can create—from MP4s that you give away to audio programs that you sell. You can create a podcast (see Chapter 13 on podcasting), a radio ad, or even your own radio show.

## TOOLS TO USE

To create an audio program, gather these four items.

1. *A hand-held digital recorder* (I recommend Sony) or your smartphone's audio record function.
2. *A general outline of the one point and the three to four sub-points that you want to share or teach in a 10- to 15-minute audio program.* Choose something that you know will be considered useful and valuable to your constituents. I recommend you use at least 16 point Times New Roman to type out the point and sub-points that you want to cover and then print it out. You can use these printouts as cue cards. It will be easy to read and you won't have to rustle papers to see the words.
3. *A simple microphone that plugs into your audio recording device.* This is totally optional. It may cost as little as $20 to $50.

4. *A coat closet in your empty house.* No kidding—the coats act the same as the egg crate foam you'd see in a fancy expensive recording studio.

## INSTRUCTIONS ON HOW TO RECORD

1. Politely invite your family to leave for a few hours. Put the dog in the yard. Unplug the phone. Drink eight ounces of water all at once.
2. Take the microphone (if you're using one), the fully charged audio recording device, a roll of duct tape, and your script into the coat closet. Sit down. Make yourself comfortable. Tape your script to the wall so that you can easily read it.
3. Pick a song you know and sing as much of it as you can to warm up your vocal chords.
4. Some people want to do a run-through. Others can speak extemporaneously off the cuff. Do it your way.
5. Press record and start speaking. Do not get all weird or falsetto or nervous. Just talk like you would talk to a friend. It's just you, those wire hangers, and the ski poles you never use.
6. If you sneeze (because the vacuum is also in there with you, listening to every word) or you choke up when you tell that emotional story, it's fine to just keep right on going. If something huge happens, like the fire alarm goes off, you may want to edit it out. Just go back to what you were saying before the minor disruption and start talking again. Don't forget to click the "Stop" button when you are done.
7. Come out into the light and do your happy dance! You just recorded your first audio!

If you deem it good enough, go ahead and upload it. If you want to improve it, spend time learning an audio-editing program. But before you do anything other than upload the file straight to a server (your site, www.Libsyn.com, www.iTunes.com, or something else) remember that, to your chagrin, most people who acquire this audio will never listen to the whole thing. Ask yourself candidly, "Is it good enough or is perfection stopping me from getting this out there?"

The benefit to you is in the goodwill generated by giving it away or selling it, not from the results people actually get from it. If you know the content is good and what you are teaching would really work if the public really applied it, rest in the knowledge that you did a good thing. You can lead a horse to water, but you cannot make it drink!

Later on, when you're making money hand over fist, you can replace this entry-level audio with one you record in a fancy studio with expensive sound engineers to help you.

# Chapter 13

# Podcasting for Profits

If you have an inquiring mind and speak clearly, chances are you would excel at podcasting. A podcast is like a radio show that you produce, but people can listen to it any time they like, and you can record it any time you prefer. There is no set schedule and the equipment you need to get started is inexpensive. All you need is a theme for your show and some good ideas.

Have you ever listened to the radio and thought, "I wish I didn't have to listen to all these ads!"? If you are like me, 99 percent of the time the ads on the radio are for things that do not even apply to you, your interests or needs. I often wonder about the advertisers—are they really taking the time to test and analyze whether their money spent on radio ads is actually converting? Or are radio ads just a strategy some marketing consultant told them to implement and no one is paying attention to see if there is a return on investment?

Imagine the difference in experience when someone is listening to a high quality, informative, interesting podcast, ad-free. At the end of the podcast, perhaps the host (you) says, "If you have just heard this podcast, you earn a promotional code! Enter the code 'WINNER' on our website and get 10 percent off all our new . . ." Or "Get our free ebook on this topic at . . ." If you just gave 15 to 30 minutes of quality content, you have earned the right to pitch. Your audience is much more likely to trust you and follow your direction because you have earned the right to pitch to them respectfully and fairly.

Stephen Woessner is the host of "Onward Nation," the fastest growing podcast in America for entrepreneurs and small-business owners (http://OnwardNation.com). Stephen also runs a digital marketing company called Predictive ROI (http://PredictiveROI.com). He uses his podcast, Onward Nation, to grow Predictive ROI, and now his podcast has taken on a life of its own.

Stephen and I met because I was on his "hit list" of ideal guests. (More on how to get guests later.) If you'd like to hear our interview, go here: http://onwardnation.com/wendy-keller/.

Stephen Woessner, host of the popular podcast "Onward Nation," pointed out that if you interview five or six people on the same topic, you could have the podcasts transcribed and edit them into an ebook. Right there, you have a new freemium!

## SIX REASONS YOU SHOULD PODCAST

According to an article sponsored by Constant Contact, "The Rising Popularity of Podcasts," (http://blogs.constantcontact.com/podcasting/) there are six reasons a business owner should consider podcasting when building a platform. They are:

1. It doesn't take much to get started.
2. Podcasts are perfect for storytelling.
3. They are extremely convenient to consume (most are only 15-30 minutes long).
4. You can become known as an industry expert.
5. Your listeners are in it for the long haul (because they subscribe).
6. You can reach a new, targeted audience.

## HOW TO SET UP YOUR PODCAST

There are three phases to setting up a podcast. Phase one is when you decide on format, phase two is when you set up your studio, and phase three, when you launch your podcast.

### Phase One: Show Format

Before you decide on your show's format, answer the following questions:

1. *Do you want to produce your show every week?* Every other week? Monthly? Don't do a daily show unless you have a clear strategy in place. Start weekly or twice a month. That will be plenty.

2. *Will you have guests?* (Most do!) Who are the top 100 people you'd like to interview? (*Hint*: choose people who have big lists to promote your interview of them to, or who are exceptionally interesting, or whose friendship could really grow your business.)

3. *What's your one specific statement?* My literary agency's statement is "We sell good books to good publishers." If I were doing a podcast for that company, that's the last thing I'd say at the end of every podcast, so people remember it. If you have a USP (Unique Selling Proposition—something that your company does to make you unique or rare in your category), put it on an index card so you can use it at the end of your podcasts.

## Phase Two: Set Up Your Studio

You don't have to start out with anything expensive. Stephen Woessner didn't. His whole setup cost just $82 from Amazon. Stephen interviews people via Skype's record feature and it works fine.

### HOW TO GET GREAT GUESTS BEFORE YOU'RE A BIG SHOT

The people with the biggest mailing lists and the most interesting companies are likely to resist being on a stranger's first podcasts. In fact, you will probably have a hard time getting guests before you've got some traction.

However, you cannot afford to start small. To "think big and act bigger," you want to pick the biggest names you can think of that you may be able to reach and then wheedle every favor you possibly can so they agree to be interviewed. It may be someone you know or it may be someone your friends or employees know.

Your ideal first ten guests should have big lists of names to which they can and will promote your podcast. Then keep moving up the sphere of influence. When you ask someone, say, "We recently interviewed [big-shot's name] and we'd like to have you on soon." Nobody wants to be first, but they all want to come to your party because of who else you've interviewed. Ask each guest, "Who do you recommend?" and then when you call that person, say, "I just interviewed your friend, and she said I should also interview you for my podcast."

To start out, you'll need the following items:

- A quality microphone (see Chapter 11)
- A pop shield that goes over the top of the microphone (about $20)
- An extender arm to move the microphone closer or further from your mouth
- Headphones that don't "leak" sound (in-ear or cupping your ears)

### Phase Three: Launch Like a Linebacker

How do you launch? First you need to arrange a time to talk with your first guest. Then do some research about your guest and prepare a list of good questions that you want to ask him or her. (Decide if you want to share the list with your guest in advance—it is not mandatory!)

Prepare yourself and your space. Put the dog outside. Shut the door to your office. Unplug the phone and turn off your cell. Get rid of ambient noise (air conditioning, forced-air heating, a fan, etc.). You don't need a swanky sound-proofed studio to do this. Take a few breaths and remember that this is your first podcast, and it's normal to make a few mistakes.

When the time comes, thank your guest, tell them how excited you are, and promise them that you will give them time to pitch their book, song, product, website, or whatever it may be at the end of the interview.

Hit record when the conversation begins. (Very important!) Relax during the interview. Pay 100 percent attention to your guest. Talk naturally, but get your questions in, unless something more interesting happens, and you find yourselves walking down a different but fascinating conversational path.

At the end of the interview, ask him or her if there's anything else you should have asked; prompt them to talk about their product or service and repeat the URL after they mention it.

Stick in your call to action—"Come to the website to get your discount code" or "Free ebook" or whatever it is that you want to pitch—and remind them when the next episode will be released. Tell them where, and how to get your podcasts. Finally, end with your USP, give the audience the hyperlink one more time, and thank them for listening. You did it! Podcast one is complete!

## EDITING: CURSE OR CURE?

What if in the middle of the podcast, someone flubbed their statement? What if during the recording, someone got the hiccups? What if you skipped a question, or you didn't like the guest's answer to something?

Should you edit?

Before you get worried about editing, though, think about how much people like bloopers on TV, or outtakes from their favorite movies. What you think is dreadful might be just fine. You get to decide, because it's your show.

## PUBLISHING AND PROMOTING

Where do you put your finished podcast? How do people find out about it? When your audio file is ready to go, you can upload it to a site like www.LibSyn.com, which hosts podcasts in the same way that Vimeo or YouTube host videos and the same way your website host sponsors your website. From there, you promote it and make it available in various distribution arenas. The website www.Libsyn.com creates the RSS feed (Rich Site Summary) that you can use to connect to sites like iTunes, www.Stitcher.com, and Google Play.

Stephen advises, "Just because somebody doesn't have a network or a platform already, or a (mailing) list already, doesn't mean you shouldn't start one. Go spend a

### HAPPY DANCE!

It's free to upload your podcast to www.iTunes.com. There is a feature called "New and Noteworthy" on iTunes. You will get immediate success if you can drive massive traffic to the first 10 or so episodes you post. That's where to put your energy in the marketing and promotion so that people will get hooked early on.

I asked Stephen Woessner how many people a podcaster needs to see consuming his or her content to know that it is working—to be a superstar on iTunes. What are the metrics?

He tossed the question back and asked me how many I think you'd need to get to the top of iTunes in a particular category. *Pause for a moment and think: how many do YOU believe you'll need?* I answered, "Three hundred to five hundred downloads to make it to the top?"

To my astonishment, he said, "Half of that!" So if you can just get 150 people to download your podcast you can dominate that space! Imagine that! Induce your mom, your five best friends, your spouse, your employees, and you only need a few strangers to download your podcast to rock it!

couple hundred bucks on a Facebook campaign, create a website, link your website to your podcast, which you have uploaded to iTunes, and use Pat Flynn's Smart Podcast Player (https://smartpodcastplayer.com). Drive people to your website, give them a great gift to open the podcast link."

## PODCASTING A SUPER-ATTRACTOR

Does podcasting sound fun but daunting? Stephen has streamlined his system so now he's spending only about four hours a week creating a daily podcast, and he works it around his schedule. He may interview three people one day and two the next, depending on his schedule and everyone's availability.

All the podcasters I know consistently describe it as the single most important thing that exploded their lead generation. Of course, we know that once upon a time in the history of American business, the cotton gin and the telegraph did similarly amazing things. But heck, you're here now. May as well take advantage of the technology that's working at this moment in history.

Stephen made this great comment: "Set the tech aside for a second, because all of that stuff is really, honestly, easy to figure out—that's where the fear comes from, so just set it aside. Instead, focus on the strategy behind the podcasting and that's where most people get it wrong. What's the purpose of doing this? Sure, to have a platform and all that stuff and have more followers and listeners or whatever. In my opinion, unless you're able to convert that into revenue, or there's some strategic transaction, then you're really missing the big opportunity."

### STEPHEN'S DAILY PODCAST SECRET

There's magic in having a daily podcast. Most people who subscribe to a podcast set it up so they can either get the new podcasts every time they are released or they can get all the ones that have ever been released on the day they sign up. This means that if you're doing 20-23 episodes per month, and someone signs up for your podcasts on the final day of the month, they not only get that day's download, but they also get the rest of the months. This changes the math! When at the end of the year you have over 240 posted episodes and someone subscribes, they would get 240-plus downloads on that day.

Stephen said he believes hosting a podcast "gives you leverage with content unlike any other platform. With a radio show, it is 'one and done.' It is a broadcast that goes out into space. Some people hear it, great. Then maybe (a few of them) go listen to it from an archive off the radio station's website or whatever. But a podcast comes right to your phone. Ford [Motor Company] is now embedding podcast players into vehicles that are rolling off the line."

Anyone can get a podcast off the website where it is hosted or your customers can download and listen to it on almost any digital device. There are even websites that just host podcasts, and most podcasts can also be downloaded from iTunes. This flexibility means your prospects can listen any time they prefer.

A podcast created for exactly the needs of your avatars, delivered when they feel like consuming your content, and featuring your promotional message, gives you a precious marketing tool. Your prospects and customers can partake not just when you are broadcasting live, but whenever they are in the mood for it. Some might listen to ten podcasts back-to-back on a lazy Sunday, and some might listen on the drive to work—two weeks after you recorded it. Podcasts stay there in the archives, remaining valuable and present to meet the customer's needs.

A well-done podcast grows its listenership with every edition. That means you can watch the analytics as more and more people—potential customers—start downloading your podcast.

## HOW TO MAKE MONEY FROM YOUR PODCAST

Once you have a lot of regular listeners, you can:

- Sell sponsorships (see Chapter 19)
- Have people pay to be interviewed by you
- Sell advertising (like a radio station does)
- Sell from the podcast (an ad at the end, a pitch during)
- Convert listeners by giving them something on your website and then having your reps sell to them directly.

There are pros and cons to each option. Think it through before you determine your strategy. There are lots of other good books out there on podcasting, and Stephen Woessner's upcoming book, *The Complete 20-Step Sales Generating Podcast System for Business Owners Who Want to Grow Revenue and Build a Nation of True Fans,* on the topic is in production as I write this. It may be published by the time you read these words.

# Chapter 14

# How to Create a Good Video

Start with the end in mind. What are you going to do with your videos once they are done? How will you promote them? How will you use them to attract business? When you know those answers, you can make wise decisions about producing videos.

- Will your video be used to post on your branded YouTube channel, your website, or another site in hopes of attracting more prospects?
- Will you use a video as a freemium to attract people or as a premium to incentivize people to buy?
- Will you use it to train or teach someone how to get more out of your product or service?
- Do you want to create video blogs (called "vlogs")?
- Will you use the video as an intro for new customers? For instance, will it be a welcome video that tells them how to access the information they just bought while giving them an opportunity to see your smiling face?
- Do you want people to pay you to view it, as one would for an online training?

Once you've decided the purpose of your video, creating it is easy.

## HOW TO FILM A VIDEO

Follow these ten steps to successfully film your video.

### 1. Record Decisions

Decide how you will record your video. You can do it on your cell phone, of course. You can also pick up a cheap selfie stick from almost any department store, office supply store, or electronic store. A selfie stick is a pole you screw onto your phone so you can hold it further from your body than you can with just your arm (unless you are an orangutan). The fancy ones come with a plug that makes it easier to press the on/off button while recording. I have a client who does several videos a week with just his smartphone and a selfie stick. If you decide to do it that way, you can skip several of the next steps.

### 2. Camera? Lights?

If you plan to do a lot of videos and you want high quality, buy a good video camera. Mine is a Canon

Short videos are much more popular than ten-minute-plus monologues, unless you're showing someone how to do something, for example, how to make an icing rose to put on a cake or how to trim a deciduous tree. It is much better and relatively easy to create lots of short videos in one huge recording session, and you may find you can use them more flexibly.

EOS Rebel SL1, and it is so fabulous I still don't know 80 percent of the things it can do! If you choose to buy a camera, I recommend you also buy a lapel microphone with a 25-foot cord (see Chapter 11) and a tripod. I got my tripod online—it folds up to about the size of an umbrella and comes in a case. I am tall, so I bought a tripod that extends the highest—I don't want the camera looking up my nose.

You also want to get yourself a three-light kit that has square lights. The three-light kits vary in price on www.Ebay.com. They're called "soft boxes," and they come with a cover that you can put over the bulbs. This will save your eyes and make the lights easier to adjust to so you get just the effect you want.

Jeff Richardson, an award-winning Hollywood cinematographer, said that most LED light kits for "regular people" are fairly similar in performance, although they differ greatly in cost and in the quality of the telescoping metal poles.

There are many excellent tutorials online about how to set up the lights and background. Look at some of the most popular videos on YouTube and you'll see the variety of ways people light themselves, how far they stand from the camera lens, and how much they move (not much in most cases!). Once you've figured out what lighting works best in your space, diagram the positions on a piece of paper so you can easily replicate what you have learned.

If you are not using a light kit (and you sure don't have to when you start!), film in the daytime near a window. Put the camera between yourself and the window so your face is illuminated but it's not so bright that it is hard to see you. You don't want

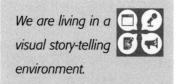

*We are living in a visual story-telling environment.*

—Jennifer Abernethy,
Social Media Consultant

to look washed out, and you don't want the shadow of the camera to be on you or your background. Viewers want to be able to look in your eyes to judge your sincerity. Humans are supremely attuned to others' facial gestures. The more that your audience can read your micro-gestures, the more you will prove your authority and sincerity.

For about $1,200, I set up an entire studio that I can fold up and store in a closet in my office. If you have a lot of money to spend, you could also rent a studio and hire a cameraman and a film editor. That's easier, but less flexible.

### 3. Where to Film

Decide where you want to film. Indoors? Outdoors? In a formal studio you create or rent? In front of something symbolic? Think about the background your audience will see. Is it interesting but not distracting? It's better to not be flat against a wall, or to have anything reflective right behind you, e.g., a piece of framed artwork. Even though you may not see the glare, the camera will, especially if you are using lights. It's difficult to record outside, where your viewers will be hearing barking dogs, airplanes, cars, sirens, children, and other people talking and because these same sounds may distract you. Unless it is part of your brand to be outside, it's probably better to do it inside a quiet space where you can control the ambient noise.

Green screens usually end up looking hokey and tend to create a fuzzy outline around the presenter. I recommend avoiding them entirely. Nobody's going to believe you're filming in Paris or on the set of a newsroom anyway. The ones that scroll to make it look like you are prancing through a field or walking through a library often resemble those fake-looking backgrounds the movie studios used to use in Cary Grant movies in the 1960s.

### 4. What to Wear

Decide what you will wear. Ever since humans stopped wearing fig leaves, we've judged others by what they wear. The guy with the leopard pelt slung over his shoulder was probably of higher rank than the shmoe who had only an ordinary antelope pelt. Think about the impression you want to make. The rule of thumb is to never wear stripes or small patterns (because they will show up blurry); solid bright red or orange (because it will wash you out when you add the effect of lights); or glittery eye shadow or lipstick. Except for Liberace impersonators and performers, nobody should wear rhinestones or other sparkly stuff, because it is unpleasant for the viewer if the light flares on it. The clothes you choose will immediately convey a message.

Light-skinned people should wear a dark contrasting color, especially near your face, especially if you will be filming against a pale or white background. Blue is always good. Consider adding a splash of a bright color, like a politician with a red tie. Darker skinned people should consider pastels to highlight and attract attention to the face. The colors will show up slightly different on different computers, laptops, smartphones, and other viewing devices.

Unless you plan to delete your videos fairly quickly, stay away from fad or trendy clothing. You don't want to look dated if someone watches your video just a year from now.

If your face tends to get oily, both genders should consider using some powder. Guys, you can pick some up discreetly from any drug store or department store. The trick is to find a shade that exactly matches your natural coloring. Don't be concerned— no one will know you're wearing "makeup" and it washes off easily. It will help you look cool and oil-free while you are filming. All newscasters and sportscasters wear makeup. It may be a good idea to hire a makeup artist on the actual day of your shoot.

### 5. How to Prepare Your Content

Are you an off-the-cuff speaker who can talk passionately after just seeing some notes or bullet points? Do you require a script or maybe even a teleprompter?

I'm in the former group, so I take a gigantic white board and write in large letters the main points I want to cover in the video I'm about to record. I hang it up just a little higher than the camera on the tripod—in the place where the eyes of the cameraman would be if there was one with me. I don't read the white board. I just glance at it to make sure I cover all my intended points in the right order. You could also use those flip charts that have sticky backgrounds and put them as cue cards on the wall behind your camera.

You can rent a teleprompter (expensive) or set up your laptop or iPad to become one. There are many different apps and software programs available; for instance, go to www.promptsmart.com.

The important detail when using notes, flip chart pages, a white board, or a teleprompter is not moving your eyes back and forth as you read the lines. Practice makes perfect! (Maybe you could write it in Japanese, so you read vertically?)

## 6. Countdown to Action

Look in a mirror before you start filming. That broccoli you had for lunch may still be in your teeth! The wind may have tousled your hair in an unflattering way. Your toupee may have slid to the left. Pretend you're on your way to the most important meeting of your life. Do you look "right"? No sparkly stuff? A dab of makeup will cover that razor nick you got this morning or that pimple you were hoping wouldn't happen. Do your eyes look awake? Take some deep breaths. Practice smiling widely.

## 7. Adjust the Camera Settings

Plug in the microphone and turn on the record function. (You wouldn't believe how many times I have forgotten to do this!) Get into position. I mark my position on the floor with a piece of tape, record a few moments of talking, replay it, and check to be sure I and my background are lit properly and focused. Delete the trial video to save space on your memory card, if you are using one.

## 8. Turn on the Record Function Again

Turn on the microphone again. Get in the right position again. Take at least one slow deep breath. Smile and count to five slowly in your head. Look right into the camera or slightly above it. Start talking. If you flub somewhere, just go back to the last point you remember and start over. Remember to smile and count before you begin again. This will make it far easier to edit.

## 9. End with a Call to Action

Make 100 percent certain you end with some kind of call to action (CTA). It could be, "Go to our website at www.[whateveritis].com to learn more" or "Get your free copy of my ebook [*title*] by clicking here now . . ." Or "To find out more, call the number on your screen."

## 10. Polishing and Profiting from Your Video Content

Now you can transfer the video to a computer or onto a thumb drive. When you're done, you can render the video through a variety of programs. We use a simple editing program called Wondershare (www.Wondershare.com). I found it very easy to learn and use.

If you feel nervous or do not want to even attempt film editing, I suggest you place an ad on www.Fiverr.com, www.UpWork.com, and on www.Craigslist.org for an experienced film editor. If you have a local film school, try there, too. Check some samples of the editor's work. When you have found the right person, you can give them the file and have it properly edited without learning any new software yourself. *Note*: always make sure you keep the original file for yourself, just in case.

Now upload it to the server, the place where the public can see it. We host our videos on www.Vimeo.com and then take the embed link and stick it on www.YouTube.com, in our www.Wishlist.com component on one of our WordPress websites, on www.LeadPages.net or actually onto a page on the website, depending on how we want our customer or prospect to see it. (There's nothing to stop you from plastering it in many places!)

That's it. That's the whole process. Yes, it is a little bit of a learning curve, but you can pick it up in a weekend. The benefit I find in having learned all this stuff myself is that now when I'm in the mood to film (usually right after I've had my hair done!) I can easily set it up and get going. I often film six to ten short videos in one session, with a wardrobe and background change in between. This method works better for me than having to schedule time in a studio and perform in front of a cameraman and a bunch of equipment, which I find either physically uncomfortable or just inconvenient.

This is how you can easily create video content. Now you can use and repurpose it however you desire.

# Chapter 15

# How to Set Up a Branded YouTube Channel

As of this writing, www.YouTube.com and www.Facebook.com are neck-and-neck in the race to see who will show more videos in a day. YouTube was the supreme ruler for a long time, and many people still turn to it to find a how-to video or for amusement.

A branded YouTube channel is a designated, named channel you set up on YouTube. That's where you put all your videos. It costs nothing. You create a banner image featuring your name, logo, slogan, or USP. People can subscribe to your channel and when they do, they will see new things that you post whenever you upload them. It allows you to keep all your company's videos organized in one place.

There are two ways to set up a branded YouTube channel—the easy way and the cheap way.

## THE EASY WAY VS. THE CHEAP WAY

The easy way? Hire someone who is good at this stuff. Your web developers are probably not also marketers so they may not be your best choice left to their own devices. When my company redesigned our website, we used www.PrimeConcepts.com to set up our branded YouTube channel, because they have better graphic sense than we do.

Before you commit to any company, ask them to let you view at least a dozen of the ones they have set up. Are those getting a lot of traffic? Do you personally find the graphics appealing? Ask the potential purveyor to tell you who does the keywords for the videos on the channel.

The keywords are the words people use to find your video. If more people search, "How to make ice cream at home" than "Making ice cream at home," and you only have it the latter way, you are going to miss a lot of traffic. Keywords are how Google knows which videos to serve to a querent.

The cheapest way? As always, do it yourself. But not all of it, because there's a good chance that "graphic design" is not your primary skill set. (I can sort of draw a good circle if I use the base of a cup to help me.) Hire out your graphics—www.Fiverr.com is on the cheap end, and it goes up from there. If you want to do it yourself, you can search "How to Build a Branded YouTube Channel" for the latest technical stuff. There are a lot of steps, but none of them are difficult.

It takes some thinking and some work to keep a channel lively and relevant. Your editorial calendar will be a great help here! When you blog on a topic, also create a video on it.

You may decide you don't want to constantly keep up with it. Recording, editing, and posting videos is plenty of work, not to mention coming up with titles, descriptions, and tags as well as rating, friending, commenting, and optimizing. You may just enjoy the creation of the videos and want to delegate the rest to someone else. There are virtual companies (look up www.123Employee.com) who feature such support for very reasonable fees.

Only put your best videos on your new channel, for the same reason you wouldn't go to an important client meeting without brushing your teeth or hair. Always include a call to action—the next step the person watching it should take. Common calls to action include, "Download our FREE ebook" or "Click here to get a discount" or "To enter to win, click here." These kinds of calls to action can move a person from a passive viewer to an engaged prospect.

## VIDEO BLOGGING

Perhaps you don't like the idea of sitting at a keyboard writing your blog. Maybe you don't even want to speak it into your phone or a digital recording device and then get it transcribed. There's a smart third option.

Consider creating a video blog, sometimes called a "vlog" for short. A vlog reaches out to your audience in a very human and personal way. I have friends, colleagues, and authors who just walk around with their smartphone. When they think of something they'd like to share with their followers, they just stop where they are and press "Record." They videotape interesting conversations with people that they're meeting; what they're doing or working on; and things that are happening at the conference they're attending. In a matter of seconds, they have a rough video loaded on their YouTube channel or website. (To see an example of a more formal how-to video blog, go to http://bit.ly/1r5nllV.)

If you're going to use your webcam's recording device, consider getting a basic lamp that extended up and down, on X braces like a shaving mirror. When you want to record, position it precisely in the middle behind your computer's webcam, which should be right in the middle of your face. Basically, imagine a line from the tip of your nose straight through the webcam and into the stalk of the lamp. Have it shine down on your forehead. (You can experiment a bit so you get it right before you hit "Record.") A regular 60-watt soft white bulb seems to offer better lighting for most skin types than halogen, in my opinion.

A vlog is a great way for you to change it up a little and not always confine your work to writing. They are a great way to make a semi-personal connection with your customers, let them see the whites of your eyes, so to speak, which in theory builds their sense of trust in you, and lets you attract new people into your fan base.

Promote your vlog in your newsletter. Put the URL to your YouTube channel in your email signature and on your business card. Refer customers and prospects to it. Use your newest vlog to answer a common question prospects ask you.

Watch the analytics. How many people watched within one day? One week? One month? What topics did they respond to the most? What questions or comments did you get? What should you be doing more of and what should you be doing less of?

One of the cool things about vlogging (and blogging) is that you are able to analyze what your constituents respond to best and then give them more of it. It is a form of frontlines market research for you.

Vlogging is a great strategy for anyone trying to build their reputation as a content or subject matter expert or an infopreneur (a person who makes money selling information).

When you start using this technique and you aggregate 10, 15, or 20 videos that you can share with people, you will see a major change in the size of your platform.

# Chapter 16

# How to Get Publicity

There is a saying, "All press is good press." I lived in Malibu, California, for more than 12 years, surrounded by celebrities who sometimes made certain that the paparazzi were conveniently tipped off just before the star made a "mistake." Being seen in public kissing someone who is not your spouse, or not wearing panties probably won't have the same positive effect on your business, but there are plenty of smart ways to use publicity to build your brand, just like the stars use it.

"Publicity" is defined as "free advertising." Publicity is when you or your company is featured in radio, print, or television, and you pay nothing for this exposure.

In addition to the DIY platform building we've so thoroughly discussed in the preceding chapters, you also have the option of getting yourself on real media. Radio, print, and television would love to have you on their shows, assuming you can adapt to their way of thinking.

A lot of people can't afford a $25,000 publicist. They can't even afford a $15,000 publicist, so they have to do the work themselves. What you're about to learn is how to do the work yourself so that you will get all the benefits of being on media without the extra expense. If you don't have a million-dollar ad budget but wish you did, publicity is your ideal solution.

## GOT AN EXTRA $67,281.48 TO SPARE?

In 2015, a quarter-page display ad in *The Wall Street Journal* would have cost you $67,281.48. The *WSJ* has about 1.5 million readers globally, and if just one percent of them bought your product or service, then . . .

But hang on a second. Even if you can spare the $67,281.48, you also need three lucky things to happen:

1. You need the ad to get noticed by a high percentage of *WSJ* readers. Most people do not buy a newspaper to look at the ads, so that's your first obstacle.
2. You need for it to be a "slow news day." If your ad randomly comes out on a day when something major happens in your country or on your planet, nobody will be looking at your ad.
3. Remember earlier in the book when I shared the adage, "Five hits make the sale"? That's because most of the time, people need to see something at least five times before any piece of marketing actually wriggles into their conscious mind. Lucky you if they remember where they saw your ad, track you down, and buy then from you. To achieve five hits in the *WSJ*, your ad spend needs to be a hefty $336,407.40. (If you can afford that, you're probably not reading this book, but your chief marketing officer might be.)

Obviously, those expensive display ads work for some companies or else the WSJ would be out of business. If they didn't have corporations ready to spend that kind of money, they would not have the funds to pay their reporters or to supply coffee in the break room.

Now, imagine Rick, your ideal customer, is commuting 30 minutes from his home in Brooklyn into Manhattan for work. He has a half hour to amuse himself on the train. Rick opens the *WSJ* and reads the articles. After all, that is why he bought the paper—to stay up-to-date on business news. He reads an article that catches his eye. The journalist has quoted you in it, just one sentence, with your name and your company's name. Happily, the journalist chose your best sentence.

Rick takes a quick photo of your part of the total article with his cell phone, tosses the paper in the trash as he exits Penn Station and heads to work. He searches online for your company when he gets to work, decides he wants to buy something from you, and asks his assistant to set about buying your product or service. Publicity made the sale.

It is a beautiful thing when the same media you would love to be able to afford to advertise in is now inviting you to share your message with their audience for free. Not only are they inviting you, but they are also tacitly endorsing you to their audience! You will be astonished at how getting publicity attracts people to your product, service, book, music, or business. You'll wonder why you didn't employ this strategy earlier.

There is a "magic halo effect" of being a media guest. It works in all media, from the two-bit radio station run out of a single-wide trailer on a farm in Missouri all the way to *National Geographic* magazine, *Time* magazine, and the television show, *The View*.

Why? Because the fact that you were smart enough to get interviewed in the media means you must be "somebody." You are given enormous amounts of credibility just by association, because most people lack the courage to even approach journalists. Your ideal customer has likely never even dared to dream that he or she might someday be interviewed in the media. It seems too lofty. But there you are—and you paid absolutely nothing for that one sentence that means so much, as opposed to $67,281.48 for that quarter-page *WSJ* ad that will be ignored by most.

One big media hit can change the rest of your life. I have lots of clients who are authors or speakers who will testify to this! My business grew faster because I was on the Anthony Robbins infomercial for years as one of his testimonials. (The one hosted by Leeza Gibbons in 1994, in case you care.) If you've also got a strong, professional-looking website, some ancillary platform components (ebooks, YouTube channel, podcasts, etc.) the media hit will be like the tide that raises all ships. When you get publicity, you get eyeballs plus credibility. Credibility equals trust, and people buy from people they trust.

## WHY SHOULD THEY FEATURE LIL' OL' ME?

Most people do not realize this, but this is a symbiotic relationship. The really big surprise about using the media to build your platform? They need you just as much as you need them.

I was fortunate to graduate high school and go to college at age 16. There was only one newspaper in the town I lived in then, rural Prescott, Arizona. I had been petitioning the manager of the *Prescott Courier* to give me a job there for years. He kept saying, "Come back when you're sixteen," so when I was first studying journalism at Yavapai College, he and my revered journalism professor Fred Stewart created the *Courier's* very first internship just for me. I was shivery with delight!

Shortly after I began working there, I was struck by two things: how much effort it is to fill a newspaper with good content every single day (I mentioned this earlier), and how many people threw themselves at the journalists trying to get anything about themselves, their business, or their interests covered. Most of them had no idea how far off they were! Some of them were obviously mentally unstable, but with a little thinking, the healthy people could have gotten their goal if they took the right steps.

I invite you to consider what it is like from the journalist's side of the desk.

Journalists have to fill an entire newspaper or broadcast every day with stuff that will intrigue and attract readers or listeners or viewers. Why? Because the more eyeballs the media attracts, the higher its advertising fees, and therefore the higher its revenues. That means the journalists get to keep their jobs. A journalist is a middle-man, balancing two interests.

Talk radio hosts have to get someone great on the air every moment they are live because if they do not, they will end up with "dead air." The producers and the hosts are always looking for great guests—people they can interview who will entertain their core audience and attract more listeners. The guest may be controversial, right in alignment with the interests of the audience, or the philosophy of the host, but as long as the guests help make it a "good show," the show will flourish.

The primary job of the host is to create content that people like or like to hate. Think of Howard Stern and the women who have listened to him, delighting in being shocked by his sexist statements. A radio station makes money in direct proportion to how many popular shows they air. This is the same for every newspaper, TV show, and magazine that wants to stay in business.

So instead of asking, "Why should they feature me?" a better question is, "Why shouldn't they feature me?" The only thing stopping you is your own doubts. All you will need is some chutzpah and a few great pitches. Once you get good at this, getting media will become easier for you every time you pitch.

Most people who do not yet have any media experience feel very nervous about this whole concept. Some try to evade it by procrastinating. Small-business owners are likely to say, "YES! I will do that—as soon as I can afford to hire a publicist." The way to make enough money to afford a publicist, though, is by getting media to attract busloads of more customers who are eager to give you their money.

Some people are shy or may just feel small, like they are part of the herd, or that they are not special—but the ordinariness is part of what makes you interesting. I learned this truth way back in "J-school" (journalism school) at Arizona State. The professor taught us this fundamental journalism principle:

"To tell the story of a war, tell the story of a soldier."

Basically this means that if a reporter writes, "10,324 people were killed in this war" readers think, "Oh, wow. That's awful!" and go on with their lives, because (thankfully) few people can imagine 10,324 dead bodies strewn across the landscape.

But if you write the story of Bill, a nice farm boy from Iowa, who was shipped out to the war zone, readers start to perk up. Now add the tragic elements—Bill left behind his sweet fiancée Stephanie and his sick granny.

The plot thickens.

By now, most people have a picture in their head of the kind of guy Bill might have been, and what his life and dreams might have been like before . . . before what? Did something happen to him during this process that changed him forever? Did he die? Come back injured? Is he missing? Inquiring minds want to know! You've built suspense with Bill, something the stark number "10,324" cannot do. We care what happens, because we can relate to Bill.

The media is about telling stories. You or your customer will stand in as Bill the soldier, as "Everyman," the protagonist, whose individual story is universal, the story of us all.

What if the reason you started your business was to overcome the harsh conditions in which you grew up? What if your first art gallery exhibit is coming up? Let's say you came from a poor home and the way you got art supplies was by working at McDonald's after school to save up enough money to go to the art supply store and buy discounted half-used tubes of paint leftover from their art classes?

What if the reason you got into selling life insurance is because you heard what happened to your mother's family after your grandfather died?

What if the reason you wrote your self-help book is to make sure no one else ever has to suffer as you did?

What if you fix cars because they were the only happy memory you have of him before your father left?

These kinds of "soldier" stories evoke emotions in people. Whether we like it or not, we are all just tribal beings. When you are bold enough to stand up in the tribe and say, "I believe in this!" or "I hate onions and here's why" or "Our customer Belinda overcame years of depression by using our special herbal formula," you are creating a rallying point of resonance. Others who feel the same will be attracted. Tell your story—or a customer's—because all stories are the same.

The right people will be drawn your story, because every single person alive has stories that define them. Yale-educated psychiatrist Dr. Carl Hammerschlag, often says,

"Getting media" can mean more than just when a professional journalist formally interviews you. Here are some other ways you can get media:

- Write for magazines, newspapers, online publications, or blogs as a contributor, op-ed writer, columnist, guest blogger, etc.
- Become the host of your own radio show or podcast
- Become a commentator on television or radio
- Become the host of your own TV show on cable or network
- Create blogs or videos that are promoted, posted, and published by other media

"People bond through stories. We are a story-telling species. We learn through stories." (You can find his book, *Kindling Spirit: Healing from Within* at your favorite book retailer.)

To draw your tribe to you—the people who will love your product, your story, your mission, your service, your work—you must first send up a smoke signal. Your smoke signal is the carefully crafted message that you build and convey through your conscientiously built platform—radio, TV, print, videos, audios, and ebooks.

You deserve media attention for two reasons: Your work has value and your story has merit. Your story is our story, because all stories are universal. Human beings are the same everywhere, millennia after millennia.

By now, you should know what to say, how to craft it, how to pitch it, how to attract journalists, and how to make sure you do such a good job you get invited back. You may think you have "a face made for radio" or you may be a natural in front of a camera. You may be so smart it will take a journalist at *Scientific American* magazine to unravel what you are saying. Good news! There is media for everybody and every media "hit" will move you, your career, your business, your product, or your service closer to your goal.

# Chapter 17

# How to Write a Good Pitch

I f you live in the United States and watch television news, you have probably picked up on differences in editorial focus between Fox News and MSNBC, for example. You may have noticed that the same people who watch reality shows about the Kardashians are usually not the same people who are also watching PBS.

There are media whose customers drive Porsches and media whose customers drive pickup trucks. You obviously will not succeed using a one-size-fits-all pitch with those two groups. Think about it: If you open up *Parenting* magazine, you would be shocked and horrified to find an article inside that would appeal more to the readers of *Playboy*. And vice versa.

Sometimes, people who are just getting started decide to throw themselves at as many media as possible with a generic press release. They send the same pitch to every breathing journalist for whom they can find contact information. That is what cheap, shoddy, lazy publicists do. One size never fits all. (Want to see a few samples of press releases? Get them for free here at www.KellerMedia.com/press-release.)

Do not waste your shot with a generic press release (pitch/story). That will only train the journalists to click "Delete" if/when they see something

## QUESTIONS JOURNALISTS ASK THEMSELVES WHEN EVALUATING A STORY IDEA

- Is it interesting?
- Who will care?
- Has it been done to death already?
- Is it a match with our audience?
- Is there anything new, fresh, or different about this take on it?
- Does it offer entertainment value?
- Does it teach something our readers are interested in learning?
- Is it about someone local?
- Is it timely?
- Is this source credible?
- Is it going to please our readers, listeners, or viewers?

from you in their inbox. The topic that you pitch to the media and your expertise on the subject you are pitching will be the major factors in a journalist's decision whether they will interview you.

Each publication has a slightly different audience, a space within the niche. That's why the content that you pitch must match as closely as possible the interests of that journalist's audience. So much frustration and even despair will result if you fail to apply this one principle!

The great news? It is fairly easy to customize one pitch to the tastes, style, and interests of many different audiences. To customize intelligently, you can use different words, stories, examples, jargon, and angles that apply to the type of audience that specific publication wants to please.

I know a man who runs a PR company quite successfully just based on this one principle. He has his clients write one magazine article and then he and his team modify it for the many niche publications to whom they submit. For instance, they might change the word "customer" to "patient" and send it to a niche magazine for orthopedic surgeons; then they change "customer" again to "downline" and send it to a niche publication serving a specific multi-level marketing company.

Not only can the words of the pitch be changed, but you can change the way you are offering your idea. Here's an example of the many ways you could slice your content if you sell life insurance and want to attract more customers by writing or recording interesting content.

- Pitch articles that are written by you on how important it is not to leave your family without money when you pass away, for publications that appeal mostly to middle-aged people who have started to realize that they too will die one day.
- Offer to guest blog on a website that appeals to parents, discussing how insurance can provide for a child's college education even if the unthinkable happens.
- Pitch to a business newspaper an article on the debts a family incurs when someone dies, and how insurance is meant to ease that burden.
- Create a column in a magazine for seniors—or a newspaper in a town where the population is older—on how leaving a nice sum to your family will help you to avoid being a burden by offsetting your burial expenses.
- Pitch the commuter radio stations on the angle that texting and driving can be lethal. If you plan to keep doing it, it is wise to also have life insurance.
- Craft a pitch on a feature story about a family that was saved because a single mother, with no money to spare, still found a way to invest in life insurance.

Nobody likes to think about dying, of course, but it's something that will happen to all of us. The same exact content—the importance of buying life insurance—can be slanted in many different ways to appeal to different groups. The pop music station is probably not going to interview you, but the Golden Oldies talk show probably will. Thinking about the types of media and the ways you can shade or parse out your message will make a big difference in whether you get the media you seek. Just a few good hits will dramatically increase your business—for free!

This is not a "I did it once and it did not work" kind of plan. You may have to pitch your ideal journalists several times before they notice you and take action. The payoff for consistent, customized pitching can be extraordinary, but like most of the big things in life, it takes some effort. You may as well stop reading this section right now if you already know you will quit if your lone pitch does not attract the attention you dream about getting.

So how do you start to think about building a good pitch? ("Good" being defined as one that results in any journalist putting you in any media.) You perk up your ears.

## EVERYONE'S FAVORITE RADIO STATION

For my internship at the *Prescott Courier*, I was assigned to "cub" (learn) under the auspices of a 27-year-old terse, raw New York transplant named Joel Millman. He was the first New Yorker I'd ever met and I was agog. I thought he was the most glamorous person I had encountered in my life.

After weeks of doing his grunt work—probably intended to make me quit—Joel finally allowed me to write a short article based on an incredibly dull city council meeting we had attended. I was so excited! I worked for about eleven hours on that short article, not more than about 400 words long. My heart in my hand, I finally presented it to the demi-god himself. I stood behind his chair sweating while he scrolled through it on his computer.

He mumbled as he read.

"Mmm-hmmmm."

Scrolling down . . .

"I see. Yes."

He got to the bottom of the page and hit delete!

I almost fainted!

He swiveled around, looked me in the eye and in his heavy New York accent, said, "Nobody gives a @#$% what you want to write. They only read what they care about."

Reeling, shocked, horrified, embarrassed, I rewrote the story. But you know what? For every book, article, press release, marketing piece, everything I've ever written from that day to this I've thought about the life-changing lesson Joel taught me that day. (P.S. We're still friends! He's at the *Metro New York* newspaper now.)

Now, I've just shared Joel's wisdom with you.

What can you glean from my life-altering lesson? Are you creating ideas that people care about? The easiest way to create good pitches is to remember this important truth:

*Question*: What is everyone's favorite radio station?

*Answer*: WIFM—"What's in It For Me?"

Just like when you want to start a business, people advise you to "find a need and fill it," the acronym WIFM reminds you to think about how information you have to share will benefit someone who is listening.

You may have an instinct for WIFM already. If you're already running a successful business, this may be second nature to you. To find out, take the simple quiz in Figure 17–1, page 107.

## WRITING A GREAT PITCH

How do you write something that is of sufficient interest to a journalist so they believe it to be of sufficient interest to their readers?

---

## The What's-in-It-for-Me Consciousness Quiz

This short quiz assesses your current level of WIFM consciousness. Choose which pitch you think would be more likely to attract a journalist.

Question 1: *You are the owner of a pet day care. Which pitch would be better?*

A: "The people in this town are terrible pet owners! Many of them leave their dogs home alone all day instead of taking them to a doggie day care. The poor dogs get lonely! For only $100 per week, my company. . . "

OR

B: "On Tuesday, the American Veterinary Medical Association released a study on dog behavioral problems. It found that most behavior problems in dogs are based on boredom. Dogs who are left alone for long periods of time often. . . "

Question 2: *You wrote and self-published your memoir. Which is a better pitch?*

A: "My name is Joan Willis. As a small child, I survived my crazy, crackhead mother beating me almost every day. I was molested frequently by her string of alcoholic or drug-addicted boyfriends. Today, I am a successful small-business owner."

OR

B: "The National Institute of Mental Health (NIMH.org) asserts that one out of every five girls is sexually abused before the age of 18, as are one out every seven boys. Early childhood sexual abuse leaves horrendous, life-altering scars on a child. There are five steps to overcoming childhood sexual abuse. I am the author of . . . and I lead workshops to help others here in [city]. People who employ even a few of the five steps discover that life can be . . . "

Question 3: *You are trying to start a business consultancy. So far, you have only two clients. Which pitch is more likely to get you picked up in the media?*

A: The [local city] chamber of commerce president Vic Bigshot recently estimated in a private conversation with me that four new businesses start in [city] every single week. The bad news? Most of them will lose money, cause a lot of heartache and stress for the owners, and close up within 24 months. There are three reasons businesses here in [city] fail and three ways to prevent such failure. . . "

OR

**FIGURE 17–1.** The WIFM Consciousness Quiz

---

### The What's-in-It-for-Me Consciousness Quiz

B: Hi! My name is Fred Jobs. I have been told I might be related to Steve Jobs, and that might be true—you'll have to ask my mother. LOL! I believe any business can become as big as Apple if they take my advice. I am a business consultant who has a lot of experience in business working for businesses, although now I work for myself as a business consultant. I can help your listeners start their own businesses and become successful if they will just take my advice about how to do business right.

*Scoring*: B, B, A are the right answers. Why? Because they are the ones focused on other people, not just you and your ulterior motive for seeking media.

---

**FIGURE 17–1.** The WIFM Consciousness Quiz, continued

Pretend you are your prospect. Put yourself in their shoes. Stand in front of the mirror and ask some questions aloud. What problem are they having that would make them want your product or service? What do they need to improve in their lives? What pain are they experiencing? "Talk" with a prospect without your intense desire to sell them something getting in the way of your listening. Then ask your real life prospects the same questions you asked yourself and see if the conversation is the same as you imagined it would be.

Now pick one major thread out of what you believe your customer most wants. That can become the basis of your pitch. Here are some examples.

#### Example 1
- Your potential customer wants to save money on heating/cooling costs.
- You sell windows.
- You pitch a story about wasted resources on Earth; climate change; how glass is made; how window technology has changed over the centuries.

#### Example 2
- Your potential customer wants to have fun this summer.
- You are a dermatologist.
- Pitch a story about how the long term effects of the sun can accelerate aging; the sun's effect on freckles, moles, and melasma; how the body makes vitamin D and why.

#### Example 3
- Your potential customer likes to eat out.

- You own a basic café, one of several in town.
- Pitch a story about the life cycle of a potato before it becomes a hashed brown; the rules for hygiene in kitchens and how they developed; a regular feature on your customer of the week; the story of cinnamon farming.

What can you think of for your own business?

## THE FIVE WS AND AN H

Another method is called "The Five Ws and an H." It is based on thinking through the questions, who, what, why, where, when, and how. Interview yourself aloud or in writing. You may want to record yourself talking.

Ask yourself questions such as:

- "Who would benefit from the information I have to share?
- Why do people shop in my store?
- What makes people buy my product online?
- What do people love about my services?
- What stories do I think of fondly?
- What kinds of testimonials have I gotten?
- How many people's lives have I improved?
- Who are the top five people in the country who talk about my topic, and what do they say? Do I agree with them? What's interesting about this?

Your brain should be whirling with ideas for pitches you could write by now, but if not, here are two more great ideas.

## PITCHING A LOCAL STORY

The easiest way to get a local story is to do something that benefits the local community. Let's say you run a small day spa in your town. Most of your customers are women between 35 and 50. You want to double your customer base next month. How do you get media attention without paying for it?

- Write a free ebook on hormonally-induced facial issues, book yourself on the radio talking about it, and then give it away on air.
- Sponsor a locals-only beauty contest.
- Go to the local high school to talk to the kids about the dangers of sun exposure.
- Go to a nursing home and give free facials to the ladies who are living there.
- Do a before/after makeover on a worthy woman living in poverty in your town.

- Pitch an article on the "Top Five Things Every Woman Over 30 Needs to Know About Skincare" for the Sunday insert.
- Pitch an article about "Skin Care Methods from History," e.g., the Victorians using lead to look pale or the Romans using urine.
- Give makeup lessons at the local battered women's shelter.

These things make you relevant in your local area. They all have "human interest" appeal. Journalists make money because of these kinds of stories. Give the journalists several weeks' notice that you will be doing something interesting or wonderful and someone will show up to cover it.

## TIE YOURSELF TO THE NEWS

One of the easiest and most interesting ways to get yourself media attention is to tie yourself to a breaking news story. Some stories recur, some are one-offs. If you can figure out even a loose tie between any topic you can comment on intelligently and the lead stories, you can wriggle into the limelight and get interviewed.

As I write this, yet another governor has been caught having sex with a woman who is not his wife. Yawn. Again? Won't these guys ever learn? But there's a gem in this ridiculously repetitious story, which at this moment is on all the major news channels. It is called "Opportunity."

In this case, obvious individuals who should be leaping all over this are people who:

- are relationship counselors;
- are seeking public office;
- are authors of relationship books;
- own restaurants where married people can come to rekindle their spark;
- own hotels, operate dinner cruises, flower shops, candy, or jewelry stores;
- have a blog on dating or marriage;
- are a doctor treating menopause, sexual dysfunction, or low testosterone; or
- are clergy in a local church.

Can you think of other angles? The spin may be thin, but it is better than nothing and worth the shot.

Why does this work? It's called the Scarcity Principle and journalistic ego. When a big story breaks, the journalists at CNN, *Good Morning America*, and other high-level national media are going to interview the people who have the best expertise in the field that the story broke in: maybe politicians, CEOs, famous authors, the head of the CDC, military people, etc.

If you're a journalist for a national news show, the big experts will take your call. You may know them personally. Some may be being paid by your company to be on call in just such a situation. If you're a little journalist in Podunk, good luck.

The local media is eager to find a "me too" interview. Suddenly, you show up. You offer this journalist, who is frantic to come up with something new and fresh on the top story, an angle that perhaps no other journalist has thought of yet. Always call—don't email a pitch—when you are showing them the bridge between the national story and your expertise. You just solved their problem and opened your own door in the process. If you do a good job, you may get invited back when nothing much is going on.

Local news done well is how ambitious journalists move up. It's what happened to Oprah, remember? If you turn out to be a great interview and the story gets picked up for syndication in many media, you could have just gotten your big break.

Give yourself a homework assignment. Watch the national news every day for a week. Practice finding a way to tie your subject expertise to a major story every day, even if you are still not brave enough to pitch yourself locally. Once you get the hang of figuring out all the angles and how you can fit in, you will build confidence and be able to write better pitches.

A little ingenuity can make something that to you may seem mundane be really interesting to others. It's all about the spin.

## CRAFTING AND REHEARSING A PITCH

Always write your pitch before you use it. Then edit it. Say it aloud. Edit it again. Shorten it. Wait two days and then repeat. These people don't know you. You are a cold caller when you're leaving a voicemail. You're a stranger when sending that email. Can you get it down to four or five sentences?

As you are writing, ask yourself, "What interests this journalist at this media location? What do I need to say to get this individual to bring me on as a guest? What can I specifically tell them I can do so they will know at once I am a great choice for their media?"

I've been on over 500 radio shows in my life. I had publicists get me about half of them, another third were word-of-mouth because the producers had heard me do well on another station. The remaining ones I got myself.

If I was going to pitch to a journalist on why he or she should write a story about, for example, the webinars I do on how to write a nonfiction book that will sell to a notable publisher (www.KellerMedia.com/webinars), I might tell the story of an author in their town who attended one of my webinars and is now published.

I might write, "One out of every two Americans wants to become a published author." That is sentence one. It is not about me. It is about their audience, reflecting an interest that they may have never considered their audience to have before. It would be even better if I could add, ". . . according to a recent Stanford study." (I don't think there is a study on this topic!) Or I might choose, "483,000 new books were published in the U.S. last year. How many of your readers are also hoping to become published authors?"

For the second sentence I might say: "My name is Wendy Keller, and I'm the agent behind 17 *New York Times* bestsellers and over 1,500 book deals worldwide." You get the point? I'm establishing my credentials.

The third sentence might say: "I propose a feature story on how your readers can become successful authors." Then I can list five steps that every writer must know in order to get published.

Then I would give them a contact number. Not just any number! I'd provide my cell phone number, but all dressed up for the ball. This trick works wonders! You tell them, "Here's my media hotline number, it's on 24/7, just for journalists." And you give them your cell phone number.

If you tell them you have a media hotline number, it looks like you're dedicated to the needs of journalists and that you're a quick responder. When a producer is in distress, they go through number after number after number and if you don't pick up or you don't respond in five or ten minutes, they're on to somebody else.

Sometimes a guest bails. Maybe the person didn't show up or they got sick or their dog died. Suddenly, that producer may have only a few minutes to find someone to go live right now. Make sure that person is you!

I was at a restaurant having lunch with a client in Santa Monica, California. My "media hotline" began to ring. It was a producer from the Rosie O'Donnell show. She had never spoken to me before, but she had heard me on a lot of other TV shows. She said in a mild panic, "Can you go live in five minutes?"

I told her I was nowhere near the station. She said, "We're just going to load your photo and your book, and we'll do it by phone." I did that interview on my cellphone in a restaurant. If you are lucky enough to have a journalist respond to your pitch, respond to that call or email instantly. Don't wait until morning. Don't wait until the next work day. Call back right away, even at two o'clock in the morning, even if you think they've already gone home. Call again when you think they will be in again in the morning.

These core concepts will help you craft a unique, succinct, and compelling pitch. You want two versions of your pitch. One is succinct, just four to five sentences long—something that can be used in a voicemail or at the top of an email.

Want to see a sample of both an email and a mail-ready press release? Visit www.KellerMedia.com/press-release.

You also want a full-page formal press release than can be mailed with a cover letter to journalists. A press release consists of four to six paragraphs that outline your story, with your name and your media hotline in the top right corner.

When possible, customize your pitch for the specific journalist or media you are pitching by showing you've read something similar he or she created. For instance you could write: "Because you wrote that great piece last December about global warming, I believe this would also be of interest to you. Did you know that two out of every three. . . "

Now you know how to pitch, but how do you find out whom to pitch to? Read on.

# Chapter 18

# Where to Find the Right Journalists and How to Approach Them

Here is a smart trick: Every single media outlet that sells advertising will have a fairly clear picture of the psychographic and demographic identities of their public. They will do everything in their power to appeal to their public—their own avatar. They'll be interested in you to the extent you match the interests of their avatars.

Most media will have on their website or deliverable via email a "rate card," which is jargon for an "advertiser's information packet." This defines everything they know about their audience (perhaps with a little hype). If your customers are their customers, you will be in harmony with the editorial people—whether or not you ever really want to buy an ad. If you craft a pitch that matches their audience, you are far more likely to get interviewed.

## THE BULL'S-EYE APPROACH

The simplest way to find ideal journalists is to think of your media strategy as a bull's-eye (see Figure 18–1, page 116). At the very center are the media you consume in your own geographic area.

You make a product or sell a service that you think is valuable. This means you are fairly similar to your own ideal customer. The easiest media

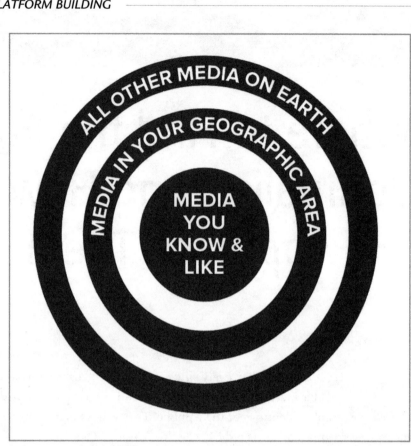

**FIGURE 18–1**. Media Bull's-Eye (Graphic by Brie Brewer, www.SquishyFox.com)

to get is the media that you already watch, listen to, and read yourself because you already know their avatar intimately; you see him or her in the mirror daily.

List the media you consume on a sheet of paper:

- What talk radio shows appeal to you?
- What local TV stations do you watch?
- What local cable shows?
- What magazines and newspapers do you read?
- Which blogs?
- What do your friends enjoy?

*Bloom where you are planted.*

—Mary Engelbreit,
Artist, Author

Now get the rate cards and ask, "Do these media appeal to my ideal customers?" If yes, they are your easiest group to pitch to.

### The Second Ring

The next ring of the media bulls eye is your geographic region. How far would you comfortably drive in one day to do an interview? I suggest you consider all appropriate media in 100 miles as "fair game." You may make the circle smaller if you live in a prime media market (Los Angeles, Chicago, New York, etc.) where there is a lot of media in your area, or larger if you live in an area of sparse media outlets (Wichita, Colorado Springs, Little Rock, etc.)

If you're on a radio show that is half an hour long, for each 15-minute segment you will only be live for 7 to 8 minutes because of the commercial breaks. In my experience, if you're on a station that directly appeals to your ideal audience, it's worth driving up to 100 miles.

You can also do a phoner. A "phoner" is radio jargon for when the radio station calls you to do the interview by phone. There's a big difference between being live in the studio and doing a phoner. The difference is in the energy of the interview. When you're in a studio, you're interacting live with the producer and the host and the other people on the team. This makes the whole thing more memorable for them and provides you with the opportunity to create a real connection with the team off air, which is valuable if you would like to come back and do it again.

### The Third Ring

The outer ring of the media bull's-eye is "everyone else on the planet." This means radio stations, newspapers, online magazines, blogs, etc., that are anywhere in the world, and whose audience avatar profile matches your customer avatar very closely. If you want to sell organic tomato seeds, the little online newsletter for people who want to run an organic farm is at least as valuable to you as the best interview you will ever get in the *Dallas Morning News* because it is tightly focused on your avatar. The more exactly your company's content, product, or service matches their audience, the more likely they are to eventually interview you, promote you, notice you, ask you to blog for them, or even to take your call.

## SO WHO DO YOU PITCH TO AND WHEN?

It's time to start pitching!

Start pitching at the center of your bull's-eye and work your way out. Do not start by pitching to *The Today Show* or CBS until you have some experience getting interviewed and some successes, so the big stations can see your other interviews and know that you are "a good guest."

The four types of journalists that you'll be dealing with are:

1. Reporters (the people who write the stories in print—online or offline)
2. Producers (the people who run things behind the scenes and usually make the decisions about who makes it onto the TV or radio show)

3. Hosts (the radio or TV front person, who may or may not line up their own guests)

4. Editors (the person who screens incoming content for magazines and newspaper online or offline)

Unless you are approaching a very small market, the host is not the person who is acquiring talent. The producer of a particular show is the one who will decide your fate.

There are two types of "stories." These are called "news" and "features." The story about the puppy who found a home after being trapped in a well for four days is a feature story. The story about how the local school board president just got caught embezzling funds meant for school art programs is news.

If you pitch a news story to a features person, you will be rebuffed in most cases and vice versa.

Most journalists get regular pitches from people like you and from publicists, and they are on the lookout for interesting stories of their own. Priority goes to pitches from publicists who have sent them interesting things before.

I got the chance to interview Laurie Allen, a top Los Angeles radio personality. I asked her how a radio show looks for a guest. She said, "The number one thing they'll look for is someone who is already in the public eye, somebody who really is popular." Like all media, she wants someone to come with a platform attached so when the radio show's platform merges with their guest, both of them grow.

But what about most people who are still trying to build their platform? Laurie said, "Have a topic that the listener would really want or relate to in a very personal way. Express it in a way that it would be desirable and relatable to everybody. Tap into their secret needs and wants."

As an example, I asked, "What about someone who may have recently published a book on how to have a happier relationship, for instance, which really is not a unique topic. How would a person spin it so they were desirable to a radio station?"

Laurie said, "Maybe ask, 'What is it you always wanted to have in your relationship?' Could it possibly be . . . and then I'd back that up with some things that you are also giving away along with it to make it really beneficial . . . like maybe [announce a contest], and the winner gets a week at your timeshare in some romantic location."

She explained that any "expert" needs to have some real examples of people who have been able to succeed using the touted methods. "Ideally, you'd have some audio clips of people talking about their results, which can be inserted into the interview. Or maybe even they can phone in to be interviewed while you are on." You can work with them in advance to develop their lines, or perhaps even hire an actor to read legitimate testimonials.

Laurie added these tips for our imaginary relationship book author. Adapt them to your topic, product, or service:

- Show us some celebrities with relationship problems and offer great solutions for them.
- Ask the host of the show, "How would you solve this?"
- Ask the listeners to call in to offer their input on a relationship challenge that a celebrity or a fictitious person is having.

When you are a great guest, every journalist in any media is going to appreciate your preparation, your personality, and your ability to be organized and to authentically connect with them and their audience. I asked Laurie to share what personality traits and conversation style have made her so engaging on the radio that she's been able to create such a spectacular career in a very difficult major media market.

She said, "I really love being on the air. I'm always having fun, and I really care about my listeners. Hopefully that's what comes through."

Do you think you'd love being on radio, too? How about this question instead, "Do you think you'd love getting tons of new customers just because you had the courage to promote yourself and get on a few radio shows or other media?"

Publicity is worth the effort and for me it is the most professional fun I've ever had in my life. You may find a whole new aspect of your career unveiling itself before you, or you may just find it is an enjoyable way to easily drive a lot more customers to your door.

## YOUR BOOKING PLAN

Start by finding 20 to 30 media outlets that you can pitch to by looking online. Because so many people ask me for help with this, I built a special page on my company's website (www.KellerMedia.com/find-media/) that shows you the big websites that collate media. As mentioned earlier, start at the inner ring of the media bull's-eye—those within 100 miles of your home. When searching online for local media, try adding the following words to the name of the towns in the area you live, such as "Little Rock newspaper," which brings up three major newspapers.

- Radio
- Talk show
- Newspaper
- Magazine
- Television
- Morning show

Next, visit the media's websites. Click their links. If the people featured on their landing page are wearing Mohawk hairstyles and covered in tattoos, and that is not your ideal customer avatar, move along.

On each site, snoop around a little. Do they interview guests? Do they have bloggers? Who is their most popular host? Is there an ad rate card you can check to see if their audience matches yours?

Before you start pitching anyone on anything, you want to know what they've done lately. This may mean reading a few issues, seeking out that journalist's name online, finding out for sure if they are truly the right person. The more keenly you target the pitch to the person you will be pitching, the greater your chances for success. The more you define and distinguish, the better results you will get. (Remember: You only have to do this once!)

If you find a journalist or a media outlet that matches your avatar, put this data about them on an Excel spreadsheet:

- Full name
- Job title
- Company name
- City
- Media type (radio, magazine, etc.)
- Phone number
- Email or email format
- Submission instructions (if found)

Keeping it on a spread sheet will allow you to track submissions and responses.

If you have the opportunity to find out something personal about the journalists or their colleagues, leverage it. Maybe while you were waiting in the green room or the lobby you found out that the host brings his dog to work and it had to be walked before you went live. Now you know something about the host: he likes dogs. What are you going to do with this information? You're going to make sure that you send a milk bone to Fido with a bow around it and a thank-you note, "Hey Bob, thanks for having me on your show. This is for Fido."

If you promised something to any of these journalists, make sure you follow through with it at once. If you said, "I'll get you my Grandma's recipe for chicken soup" because the host was getting over a cold when you were in studio, follow through as if this person was your new best friend.

The people you meet in one media location likely know everyone in their market and could refer you to others. You are there to give a great show, make new friends, and get your message across.

Our very impressive, extraordinarily well-connected client, Judy Robinett, wrote a book called, *How to Be a Power Connector*. If you have been less than great at making and keeping interpersonal connections so far in your life, grab a copy and read it.

# Chapter 19

# How to Get Sponsors

You've seen racing cars with manufacturer's labels plastered all over them. You've seen cyclists, surfers, and runners with labels on their bodies or on the equipment that they use while being televised. All of those are sponsorships. For years, one popular romantic TV sitcom superstar was on commercials talking about the home hair coloring product she claimed to use. Do you really think she was dying her hair at home? Me neither.

All of these are called "sponsorships," and you should have a piece of this flow! There are sponsorships you may not have even thought about. The local construction company buying uniforms and equipment for a Little League team is a sponsorship and when the dry cleaners and the clothing boutique co-promote one another, that's a type of sponsorship, too.

Your small business could grow exponentially if you finagle a sponsorship. Think about this carefully before you toss this idea away. Sponsorship is when you get a company to help you make more money. It can take a variety of forms, such as when a company:

- promotes your product or book to their customers for you;
- uses your freemium or premium when they sell their own products;
- pays you to be their spokesmodel or spokesman because you are seen as a person who has influence with their customers;

- pays some or all of the costs associated with a promotion, product, or service you have (for example, a book tour);
- gives you gear or equipment;
- gives you consumable goods (food, hair spray, etc.);
- gives you something with their name on it to give to your employees or customers or to stick in a gift bag at an event you sponsor;
- pays for all or part of an event or promotion you produce; or
- advertises you or your business to their people.

For example, I worked with Cherie Calbom, known as "The Juice Lady." This was in the early days, before the juicing craze began. If you watched the infomercials selling the Salton Maxim juice machines back then, you likely saw Cherie stuffing carrots and celery into the "Juice Lady Jr." juicer. She has a perky personality, a great smile, and a nutrition degree from Baylor University.

When Cherie asked me to sell her book to a publisher, she was already the spokesmodel for the Salton Maxim juicers. But the piece that got the publishers salivating was that Salton agreed to give a copy of the book to anyone who bought the juicer within a certain time period. As in, "If you buy in the next 10 minutes, you'll get this book for free!" It was their premium. This sponsorship made a huge difference in the advance I got Cherie from her publisher.

## IDEA SPARKS

See if any of these spark ideas for you:

- I helped a client who wrote a book on barbecuing. He got paid a lot of money to do a multi-city tour for a major American alcohol manufacturer to promote their new liquor line as a main ingredient in barbecue sauce recipes. Another company gave his book as a premium every time someone bought one of their fancy grills. A chain store featuring outdoor goods sold his book in their stores via non-trade sales. (Any book sold outside of bookstores and other traditional book vending places is called "non-trade" sales.)
- I had another client whose book and expertise in bioterrorism helped him successfully obtain more than $150,000 in annual sponsorships and grant money for an NPR radio show he launched and co-hosted.
- A woman I consulted had written a book on children's birthday party planning using candy sold by a famous candy company based in most American malls. She pitched them on selling the book next to the cash register in their stores.

- A man I consulted wrote a book on how lawn care is a great fitness activity for men, and how to burn extra calories while doing it. He approached the major seed and garden supply centers to distribute and promote his book.
- One of my dearest friends works for a company that manufactures clothing for people who work in healthcare. Turns out, the manufacturer pays any successful blogger (nurse, doctor, or other) in the healthcare world to mention them or allow them to post ads on their sites.
- One of my clients runs business conferences. Those can be very expensive to market, rent the room, and get the catering, pay for signs and good speakers. A 120 percent of his costs are regularly paid by companies that also want to get in front of his specific attendees—all business owners. He makes money every time he puts on an event, before he even starts counting the income from ticket sales.
- A girlfriend had previously owned a beauty salon, which she turned into a string of successful spas. She was hired by a multi-level marketing company to be the spokesmodel for a line of skin care products targeted toward middle-aged women. She earned hundreds of thousands of dollars. All she had to do was consult them on the colors used in the packaging and appear at the company's big events talking about "her" line and how wonderfully it worked.

Before you start salivating over the ideas spinning in your head right now, let me tell you this stark truth: it's not like you're going to pick up the phone, call a multi-national company, ask for the CEO, and pitch your great idea.

There are steps you'll need to take, and in my extensive experience of working with people who are pursuing sponsorship opportunities, the odds are about 1 in 30. That is, for every 30 companies you work (hard) to get a sponsorship deal with, you are likely to get one sponsorship. And it may not initially take the form you wanted it to. They may not give you a check for $25,000 to pay for your marketing campaign or put you on stage at their national conference—they are corporations. They think differently than entrepreneurs do, so decisions usually take longer and require more approvals, and have a longer testing cycle before they're ready to risk their reputation. (Hint: consider working with entrepreneurs first to make this process easier!)

## HOW TO GET SPONSORSHIP DEALS

I've been in and around more sponsorship deals than most people. I have some great insights into what I've seen work, but my experience and expertise pales in comparison to that of Ryan Blane, creator of the Get Sponsored Fast program—www.

GetSponsoredFast.com. Lucky for us, I was able to interview him and get you some solid answers to how sponsorships really work.

Ryan says there is a big opportunity opening in the world of sponsorships and it comes through the power of social media. (See Chapter 10.) Ryan says, "A lot of times people think of using the technology of social media just to reach their own audience. Not only does social media let you reach your audience, it also lets you understand them a lot better, both in terms of watching your analytics (seeing how people are responding to what you're saying/posting) but also demographics—understanding who your audience is, where they are, what they're really thinking about. Who is actually visiting your sites and interacting with them?" In other words, know your avatar and how to reach them!

If you have created an actual conversation with the people who drop by your social media, you are getting to know them. When you know them, you can identify them. When you know their interests and needs, then you have the opportunity of finding others who can fulfill their needs and interests in whole or part with you.

Ryan consulted with a company that makes scrubs for nurses. This company looks for nurses who are successful bloggers. The manufacturer knows that the people who read those blogs are primarily nurses, so they buy banner ads on the bloggers' sites and may even incentivize them to review their products favorably. It's a perfect match.

People who buy juice machines or barbeque grills are going to need some great recipes. People who buy high-end designer clothes are certainly going to need a good, reliable dry cleaner. If you are blogging about juicing for health; raising beef cattle; or running a modeling school, your potential sponsors are everywhere.

Why would a company even consider partnering with you, just because you have a growing social media presence? Because they have a problem. A successful company may have hundreds of thousands of customers, but the customers might trust what you say about that company long before they would trust what the company says about itself. The customers may be choosing between buying from one company and another. You as a blogger, author, vlogger, or video provider may be the person they like and trust, so you may be more valuable to the company than they can be to themselves.

Ryan said, "Of course, it's not just social media that matters. Any time you can aggregate and influence an audience, you are primed to attract a sponsorship opportunity." This means, as you build your platform, attracting your avatars, other people want you (just like you want media). It is a reciprocal agreement. Dr. Carl Hammerschlag, whom I mentioned earlier, recently put on a public health event near his home in Scottsdale, Arizona, called "Clown Town Healing Fest." (www.ClownTownHealingFest.com). He got sponsors from a regional medical school (University of Arizona) as well as lots of media. As people saw the big sponsors and the media, regular people and smaller businesses started to climb aboard. He got hundreds of people to contribute money, time, or products. He attracted exhibitors. Naturally, crowds of people attended, which not only brought benefit to the Healing Fest, but also to all the sponsors he had collected. The sponsors and Dr. Hammerschlag were able to meet new prospective customers and clients, people who might never have connected without the event to bring them together.

Ryan asked, "So if you create a video and it gets thousands of likes, what does that signal to a potential sponsor? That you've got the ear of their future customers."

"The more visits you have, the more eyeballs you get, and the more times they come, whether it is to your social media pages or your website, the more power you have to attract sponsors."

## HOW TO FIND LIKELY SPONSORS

Let's assume you have a following—online or otherwise—that you can prove. (Your website traffic can be easily tracked, there's no room for fluff!) "The first thing to do is put your sponsor hat on," Ryan says. "Look at your business or look at what you're offering to a sponsor. Ask yourself, 'What does the sponsor want?' Look at what their needs are. For sponsorships, the first thing they'll want to know is, *'What's in it for me?'*" (Ha! Does that WIFM sound familiar?)

First, you'll need to compile all your stats. How many people interact with you on:

- Facebook
- Twitter
- Pinterest
- LinkedIn
- Instagram
- Periscope
- Your website
- YouTube channel

When you have these stats, you'll know which companies are likely to sponsor you, but also how high you can go up the totem pole. Ryan used the example of a dirt bike racer. "If you compile your stats and on top of that, you're also out travelling, and you're riding in stadiums in front of 10,000 people a month, put those numbers in as well."

For anyone regularly doing media interviews, speeches, or workshops, add in those audience numbers, too. Ryan suggests, "Your job is to compile a clear picture that says to the sponsor, 'Here's the number of people you can reach by becoming involved with me.'

"You are basically saying, 'OK, collectively you can reach an extra 110,000 people this year by sponsoring me. Those people are 60 percent male and 40 percent female. Their average income is $110,000 per year. They are mostly college educated and they own their own homes and have 2.8 children.'"

What's your total number? This kind of data is the stuff corporations and large companies feed on. You can approach companies whom you believe should sponsor you at a regional, national, online, or whatever type of level only after you figure out precisely how many people you can deliver. *Hint*: as you grow your platform, this number increases.

Next, ask yourself, "Which companies also want to reach my audience?"

## HOW TO PURSUE POTENTIAL SPONSORS

Obviously, someone who can bring a few thousand people is unlikely to attract a multi-national company as their sponsor. Ryan said, "Let's go to the sports reference. If someone is just starting out in their sport and they don't have a championship under their belt or they don't have a lot of big things yet, I recommend they not approach Red Bull while they are still at [entry] level because Red Bull is going to ignore you."

So being realistic is part of the process of increasing your chances of getting a sponsor. "The best place to start is the people you're already doing business with . . . they might not give you cash, but they could give you other things that are valuable," said Ryan.

Ryan said, "It's really boot-strapping your way up. Once you get a big sponsor, it's easier to get a lot of relatively small sponsors involved. The smaller ones think, 'Oh! If they're involved, we want to be involved, too.' This helps you not only get more and equal sponsors, sometimes larger ones, but definitely expands your audience, too." That's just like what Dr. Hammerschlag did with the Clown Town Healing Fest when he got the University of Arizona medical school as an anchor sponsor.

Some of it is a little magic sauce, too. When I first opened my literary agency in 1989, there were no certification programs for new agents, so I read biographies of earlier successful people in my industry. One memorable book was a biography of super-agent Irving Paul "Swifty" Lazar (1907–1993). Swifty was renowned for pitching a famous actor on being in a film he wanted made. Of course, every good actor would reply by asking, "Who is the director?" Swifty would tell them and then he'd hustle off to that director and say, "Listen here! I've got (that famous actor) interested in the film. You want in?" Then he'd go back to the original actor and say, "Like I said, that director is on board. You want in or don't you? Decide now." And so forth, building the enthusiasm and commitments as he went along.

Think of Swifty's model as you're building up to those multimillion-dollar sponsorships. You may have to swing from branch to branch, but you'll get there if you keep growing your platform.

## STRUCTURING A DEAL

Most people approach sponsorships thinking, "I just want some corporation to write me a check for $25,000." You maybe don't have a big enough platform yet. But there may be 25 deals worth $1,000 each if you open your eyes and look around. There are all kinds of creative ways to structure a new deal in ways that allow the partners to get to know one another, see if it really benefits them both, and move forward slowly.

Here are some ideas for deal structures:

- Ads or signs (online or in a location)
- Discount coupons (perhaps going both ways—they give away coupons to you, you do the same for them)
- Percentage of sales (I personally am involved in a large number of these types of deals. They call it "affiliate deals" in the online world)
- Product or service gift or exchange
- Sponsorship for signage
- Co-operative awards (you all contribute $X to an award, contest, or event and then you all promote the event or award—see Chapter 20 for more details)

## THE SPONSORSHIP PROPOSAL

Start by looking at companies that are already sponsoring others. When you've compiled the target list, it's time to build what Ryan calls a "sponsorship proposal." A sponsorship proposal highlights what you have to offer them (your audience, primarily) and then asks for what you need, in a fairly specific way. You want to make sure you keep the focus on the benefits to them. Assemble your numbers and make your approach. For more examples visit Ryan's site at www.GetSponsoredFast.com.

# Chapter 20

# Contests, Raffles, and Giveaways

You can also apply what you've just learned about sponsorships to the idea of giving things away via contests, raffles, and giveaways. There are two reasons to consider doing something like this. First, these attract a lot of attention because people love the idea of getting something for nothing. Second, they create fanfare that you can use to get media.

The main reason businesses like yours do "contests" (which is the word I will use for the whole shebang in this chapter) is because it attracts a flood of new customers. It sticks your hand up and waves it wildly. The more people who know about your contest, the more people who know about your business. A percentage of those who find out about your business in this way will be interested in finding out more, even if they didn't win a prize.

The net effect of these kinds of big, splashy things is that it makes you more memorable, as someone who does interesting, refreshing things in your industry. The process itself is easily replicated and modified once learned, and it will give you a quick marketing strategy you can keep in your back pocket when you need to refresh public awareness that you and your business exist.

## STEP RIGHT UP, LADIES AND GENTS

A "Contest" refers to an event in which people compete.

A "Raffle" is a way to raise money by selling tickets that if chosen, win a prize.

A "Giveaway" is when participants get something just for showing up or taking another common action.

All of these could be turned into interesting, attention-grabbing, innovative, and inexpensive ways for you to generate some great new business.

## CONTEST TO-DO LIST

Here's a checklist for putting a contest together easily. Make sure you give yourself plenty of promotion time, since promotion is the true purpose here. I recommend at least two months.

- ❑ Choose what kind of a contest, raffle, or giveaway you want to run.
- ❑ Decide if you will pursue sponsors to donate prizes, help spread the word, or help in other ways.
- ❑ Decide what you want to give away (more than one prize means more media and promotional opportunities).
- ❑ Check to see if there are any legal issues where you live.
- ❑ Decide how long you want to give people to "earn" it.
- ❑ Decide how entrants could win.
- ❑ Decide how you will promote the heck out of it.
- ❑ Decide how the prize(s) will be awarded (*Hint*: fanfare is a great way to get even more attention from prospects, maybe media, and current customers).
- ❑ Get graphics designed.
- ❑ Choose your launch date.
- ❑ Promote the heck out of it!

## POTENTIAL PRIZE IDEAS

Here are some potential prize ideas:

- ■ Money

- Gift cards for your product or service
- A makeover (for them, their house, or their car)
- A car or other expensive object related to your business (a plumber might give away a new washer/dryer set)
- A trip (do you know someone or do you have a timeshare sitting unused somewhere interesting?)
- Services (free dry cleaning for a year, a website CEO review)
- A certificate or plaque (usually accompanied by a chicken dinner and women wearing cocktail dresses)
- Scholarships
- Tickets to something related (sports, opera, a flight, etc.)
- A trophy (the bigger the better)
- Representation (legal, artistic, modeling, etc. My agency has done this a few times with varying degrees of success. Warning: you will have to choose a winner, even if none of the entries thrill you!)
- Objects (a television, a laptop, a suit, a quilt, etc.)
- Information products (your book, CD, etc., although these usually pull far fewer prospects than all the other items listed above)

In some states, counties, or cities, contests are governed by laws. Mostly, these laws are there to ensure you do not sell raffle tickets and then not award a prize to anyone. Make certain you check with your local authorities before you do this.

What other ideas can you come up with? If you offer one grand prize and a few smaller ones, you'll attract more people because more people will believe they have a chance of winning.

## GETTING YOUR PRIZES FOR FREE

You do not have to go out-of-pocket to acquire the prizes you will be giving away (unless it is cash). You can:

- Barter your services with someone who has something that would make a good prize.
- Get a wholesale license to acquire goods cheaply.
- Trade in your bonus points earned on a credit card to get a valuable object.
- Trade in your frequent-flier miles to award airfare or a hotel stay.
- Give away something you already have.
- Negotiate with another non-competing vendor who wants the same customers.

- Offer to include another business as part of the contest and split the costs.
- Get someone to donate the prize to you so you can give it away.
- Get sponsors.

Why would anyone want to sponsor or donate stuff to your contest? Because you have the energy and the smarts to even think of doing a contest! Your innovation alone will attract peers who want to get a piece of your enthusiasm for their own business marketing. If they are donating or sponsoring it, perhaps they will also mail the announcement to their list, post signs in their store, hang a banner off their building with your contest website on it, all in return for you putting their logo somewhere on your promotional materials.

## HOW WILL PEOPLE WIN?

- You can sell tickets and host a public event where you or a girl in an evening gown or the mayor swish them all around and select a few winners.
- You can ask people to send in a video telling the world why they love your product or service, your book, your music, your painting, anything. (Make sure you have them sign a release upon submission that lets you use it any time and place you want—in some states, this can be digital.)
- You can ask them to write something for you—an essay, a short story about how they used your product, or a story about how their life changed when they used your services.
- You can ask them to create a collage and email a photo of it.
- You can ask them to create an artwork.
- You can ask them to submit something that is typical in your industry. For instance, my agency has asked for book proposals. A modeling agency I worked

All office supply stores sell blank certificates you can use to create the awards you'll be giving away. Buy yourself some blue ribbon, some gold foil seals, and a diploma holder and voila! You have a tasteful award certificate anyone would be honored to receive.

Whatever way you choose to award the people, you must immediately deliver on the prize promised. Market the contest, the prize-giving process, and the immediate post-prize awarding aggressively. You may be surprised how large your list grows via this simple and effective strategy.

for as a teenager asked everyone to submit their head shots.

- You can ask them to send photos of themselves using your product in strange places, e.g., reading your book while rappelling off a cliff.

The possibilities are limited only by your imagination. You can be the judge all by yourself, or you can use the prestige of the judges (local or national celebrities) as an asset in your contest marketing materials. That's why the TV show *America's Got Talent* used celebrities, not music teachers or record label producers, even though ostensibly those people would have been better qualified judges.

## HOW WILL YOU AWARD THE PRIZE?

The attention from prospects and hopefully media that you will get just for having the contest is one thing. The actual act of awarding the prizes is another opportunity in itself.

If you can afford it and the prize is big enough, the tried-and-true event is always best. Think "red carpet" and host an elegant sit-down dinner. Be sure to invite prize winners and a few of their family members, the mayor, anyone who really helped you promote the contest, all the journalists who covered it, and anyone else it would be politically expedient to invite.

You can also bring the winner into your office, get some balloons or flowers, hand them a certificate or a big cardboard check, and take a lot of pictures that you plaster all over social media.

You can even just sit in your home office by yourself and email/call the winners to let them know they've won and announce it on your social media that you've given something to someone you've never seen. This last option is least fun but is also the least expensive.

# Chapter 21

# Using Workshops, Webinars, and Seminars

I f you have even an ounce of "teacher" or a dash of "performer energy" in your blood, you may enjoy using live events as a way to build your platform. This can be a fun, relatively easy way to get a lot of new business fast, and it doesn't have to take a lot of money.

## MAKING MONEY BY GOING FREE

Jeff is a grief counselor. He does free events in the spare rooms of churches, libraries, and other public spaces a few nights a month. His events are promoted by the place giving him the free meeting space, plus he places announcements for his regular programs in the calendar sections of the local newspapers.

When you attend his events, you find out what a comforting, understanding guy he is. Plus you get a chance to see that the few simple ideas he shares during the free event really make a difference in the way you feel. It makes you far more likely to sign up for his paid grief counseling program. Last I knew, he was making about $100,000 just from using this kind of marketing.

Daven Michaels runs several large businesses and is a successful marketer, author, and professional speaker. One of his companies is www.123Employee.com. They provide virtual assistants to companies all over the world. I got to know Daven and then represented his book (which became a *New York Times* bestseller), *Outsource Smart*. Daven likes to travel, so when he was growing his company, he went around the world offering free live programs on time management for entrepreneurs. Surprise! The answer to finding more time is to delegate better to his team of well-trained virtual assistants.

A chiropractor near my home offers the occasional program on getting over lower back pain. Did you know lower back pain is one of the most common complaints that (big surprise) leads people to seek out the services of all chiropractor?

Chances are, you are seeing a theme here. How can this apply to you?

## TYPES OF PRESENTATIONS THAT PRODUCE PROFIT

There are several types of speaking engagements that work for small business owners.

- *Workshops*—where people actually engage with the speaker(s) and do something, like build a marketing plan or paint a picture or learn how to use QuickBooks online. This could include a support group, like you'd expect from a therapist or life coach.
- *Seminars*—where one or more people lecture other people—sort of like high school. You might call it a "talk" or a "program" or a "training."
- *Speeches*—where one person is brought in to speak to others on a topic of specific interest, but there is a whole program and the speaker is not the only event. For instance, there could be a meeting or a meal or something to go with it, like you'd expect at a national conference, a monthly meeting, or at a rally. Speakers are often paid for their services, the most common fee being $5,000 per event. I teach programs that help people learn how to get paid to speak for money. This helps me and helps the registrants. Visit www.KellerMedia.com/webinars.
- *Webinars*—a seminar delivered online, usually through the services of www. GoToWebinar.com or a similar provider. An unlimited number of people tune into a website URL and listen and watch as you present. In some cases, they can see your face. In others, they can only see your slides. Lots of options, lots of money to be made.

## HOW TO CHOOSE YOUR IDEAL TOPIC

Of course, the trick to success is picking a topic that proposes to solve the biggest problems your future customers are facing. Finding and clearly describing the benefits (ideally in the title) is a big part of getting people to attend live or online. Consider what solutions you might offer to individuals who show up.

The other part of the puzzle is what you can speak about successfully. I've taught more than 8,000 entry-level speakers, and I always challenge them to ask these questions of themselves:

- On what topics do I have both expertise and passion?
- Have I established that complete strangers like the way I talk about those topics (usually via blogging, related videos, webinars, media, etc.)?
- How fast is my platform growing? (Less than 10 percent per month? Tweak your topics.)
- Can any of my topics be adapted for a business audience? That's where most of the money is in speaking!

> More people show up at 6:30 P.M. local time on a Wednesday or Thursday evening than any other option. Test what works best for you, but do start there.

*Warning*: If you have not yet proven your topic and tested that the way you phrase the benefits that you promise are appealing to your public, you are not ready to pursue a live event. Test it repeatedly on social media before you invest copious energy in a live event.

## PUTTING ON A WORKSHOP OR SEMINAR

Once you have clarity about your topic, a bit of a following in the subject matter, and you decide that you want to put on a workshop or a seminar with a live audience in an actual location, there is something you should know: There are some significant, scary pitfalls ahead. They are:

- What if no one shows up?
- What if no one who shows up buys anything you're selling?

You're going to want to minimize your risk before you start promoting your program. There are a couple known ways to lose money. (This is the voice of harsh experience!) Here are some cautions to heed.

### The Seven Cautions and the Seven Precautions

The cautions and precautions are tricks that seasoned presenters use. You can use them too and save yourself from some drama and stress.

#### Caution 1: The Venue

If you are renting a room, the venue usually requires you to put down a deposit to hold the space. This means that whether or not you get people, sell tickets, or sell products, you already paid them a non-refundable deposit. It's not like a hotel room where you can cancel the day before (in most cases). Note that their money is made largely by whatever catering you provide. This is often the most expensive part of the event, and sometimes a venue (event location) will give you the room for free if your catering budget is big enough. If you pre-order lunch for 12, you cannot change it if only six people show up. Usually, you cannot bring in food from the outside. Ask lots of questions before you sign the contract.

### Caution 2: Space and Seating

If you rent a room for 100 and only 10 people show up, it is going to be uncomfortable and embarrassing. If you rent a room for 20 and 200 people show up, it is going to be a hassle, scrambling to fit them all in, find more chairs, and even stay within the fire code regulations.

In major cities, you are unlikely to have a problem if you take whatever number of people RSVP and plan on 50 percent of the people showing up.

In small towns, the opposite is likely to happen. Since there are fewer distractions in rural places, it is not unusual to have 10 to 15 percent more people show up than registered. Unless you state it clearly otherwise, people may bring children, spouses, pets, or relatives.

### Caution 3: More Parts Means More Problems

When you are starting out, keep it simple. If you are planning an all-day event with catering, multiple speakers, and at a venue that is a distance from your home, I strongly urge you to start smaller and practice. If you plan to use a spectacular PowerPoint presentation with embedded video files, internet access, and music, you are setting yourself up for problems until you know exactly how to set yourself up. Arrive at least four hours early for a run-through.

### Caution 4: Attendee Shrinkage

If you are boring, monotone, read your notes continually, don't engage the audience, or start pitching before you have delivered great value, people will walk out.

I've given around 600 presentations and trained about 8,500 people to become paid professional speakers so far in my life (for information, go to www.KellerMedia. com/webinars). My very first speech ever was at a community college. I was more than eight months pregnant with my third child. The sponsor told me to plan on a two-hour evening program for adults. I carefully wrote out and practiced that program and its timing so it would be exactly two hours. On the big night, I was nervous. I waddled into the classroom and saw about 20 writers eager for my alleged wisdom. It was kind of scary! I said hello, sat down, pulled out my notes and started reading. Precisely two hours later, I looked up. Three people were still in the room!

If you do not have speaking skills naturally, I recommend some training. It will help you feel more comfortable, it will engage your audience better, and it will result in more sales.

### Caution 5: Get the Money

If your purpose is to sell the audience something at the end, bring change for those who will pay cash and ideally, another person to collect the money. There is also a device called a "Square" that attaches to a cell phone and allows you to swipe credit cards on the spot (find out more at https://squareup.com). Do not ask people to put their credit card info on a piece of paper. That no longer works in the world of identity theft. The more payment options you provide, the easier it will be to make money at the event. This frees you up to chat with prospects.

If your purpose is to enroll customers in your product or service at some future date, be sure to have handouts with your contact info on it and perhaps a discount coupon with an expiration date. Collect names and contact info as people enter the room—this is often why an event has a sign-in sheet, so the organizers can follow up and close the sale after the event.

### Caution 6: Spectacular Support Relieves Stress

As the event is about to begin, it is extremely useful to have someone you know and trust running around helping with logistics. This can also be the same person who handles the sales later. What if a handicapped person shows up and seating has to be shifted? What if four extra people show up and someone has to run to the venue manager and request more chairs? Imagine halfway through, someone starts really coughing hard and distracts the audience. If you have someone who can bring them a cup of water, you will not have to attend to them from the stage. Imagine you are going to use a PowerPoint presentation and suddenly, the projector is not working or you did not bring an extension cord long enough for your laptop—it's good to have help.

### Caution 7: Dealing with Your Nerves

If you are human, you are bound to be nervous—or at least jittery—as the event begins. Preparation is critical to allow you to focus on giving the most benefit possible and being as relaxed as you can be. Go over your intended program from greeting to closing at least three times in the days preceding, even if you plan to speak off the cuff. It will improve your flow and improve the experience for your audience, and increase your sales.

## Solving the Venue Issue

The easiest way to get burned doing live events is to follow the hotel's rules and put down a big advance on the room, but then not make your money back from the event. This stings like nothing else. I have had events that made a huge amount of money and ones where I have lost money. I will warn you about this: if you are charging for admission and you start your presentation knowing that you are working at a loss, it is super hard to get motivated and give your best, and people who have chosen to take their time to attend any event of yours deserve your best.

I have a solution that I have taught to my consulting clients and authors. Now I'm sharing it with you—please keep in mind that everyone's experience will be different.

If you are holding a live event and you believe you will have 50 or fewer attendees, you can likely wait to book your venue until the last minute. This only works if it is a one-day or less event, not if they have to stay overnight.

1. Plan to hold your event in an area that has a large number of suitable hotels or other venues with meeting rooms of varying sizes.

2. Use a registration form on your website. When someone registers, give them the general area in the town in which it will be held, but not the specific address. In the registration confirmation email that you send immediately, state "You will be given exact location and parking details 10 days before the event. This is a precaution against 'party crashers' at our popular program."

3. Fourteen days before the event, you will likely have 50 to 60 percent of your total registrations in. If this is a paid event, plan for twice as many as you have that day. If it is a free event, even though you may get a lot more registrations between now and then, you probably won't actually get many more attendees to actually show up. There is usually a surge of last minute registrations in the week before the event.

   Now start calling hotels and meeting spaces to see who has a room available for that number of attendees. Make an appointment to go tour all those venues as soon as possible. When you meet with the meeting planner in person, negotiate hard on price. Nearly 99 percent of the time, the meeting rooms are about to go to waste.

   Almost no one has the guts to do it the way I've just described, so anything that isn't already booked for that date is highly unlikely to book and the venue sales person knows it. Any money is better for the hotel than no money, so you will find them more accommodating and willing to negotiate. Try to get them to agree to hold the space for you with only half or less money down. (Unsure about your negotiation skills? May I humbly recommend you read a copy of my book, *The Secrets of Successful Negotiation.*)

## THE EMERGENCY KIT

I have learned to take the following things to every single live event I put on. I recommend you take these with you. I use a rolling suitcase to transport my emergency kit to the meeting room.

- A liter of your favorite water and a real glass
- A few hard peppermint candies for your throat, although many speakers swear by slippery elm lozenges from the health food store (in my imagination, those taste like licking the floor in a train station!)
- A 12-foot industrial style extension cord
- Brightly colored duct tape that removes easily from carpet (for holding down the aforementioned extension cord so no one trips, and you don't get sued)
- Your entire PowerPoint presentation on a thumb drive (if I'm using one)
- Spare battery pack for your laptop, fully charged, even though you'll be using a power cable
- A bandage and some antibacterial ointment
- A small package of tissues
- A large, inexpensive wall clock. (I hate it when speakers look at their watches or phones to determine where they are in their program, so I use a pushpin to put it somewhere at eye level so I can glance at it without being obvious to the audience.) Take out the battery and tape it to the back of the clock when not in use.
- Two pushpins (one of which is used to hang the clock)
- Spare pens and a permanent marker
- A full set of dry erase markers and a full set of flip chart markers, each one labelled with your company name on it
- Sufficient handouts and a copy of your slide printout in a plastic folder or case so nothing gets crushed
- Filming or recording releases for each participant to sign, if relevant
- Transparent tape
- Directional signs with arrows (left, right, straight ahead, room X), the name of the program and your name on them. Hotels often dislike us to use them, but if they didn't put the right directions on the marquis, or if it is easy to get lost on the way to the room, you'll be glad you have them with you. Use them to direct traffic. I

**THE EMERGENCY KIT,** continued

often take a few others that say "Shhh! Program in session!" and hang it on the door when the room is still filling up. That way, when the door is shut, late comers know to enter quietly. I keep mine in a plastic envelope I got at an office supply store.

■ Slide advancer and a spare battery for it (get at any office supply store)

■ Props (people wake up when you use props).

4. Find out about parking, make your catering decisions (if any), ask what the venue is willing to give you (e.g., pens, notepads, candy at each place setting), and tell them how you want it set up. I always choose what is known as "classroom style" if I expect fewer than 30 people. That means banquet tables that seat two people each. It seems to make the audience more comfortable to know they can stow stuff under a table and get up to go to the bathroom easier.

5. Now you can at last tell your attendees where to go. Make sure you include the instruction, "Please do not share this location information with anyone!" which subtly carries on your theme of trying to prevent party crashers.

I've saved many thousands of dollars doing it this way. It may not work if you are trying to hold your event in an area that only has two to three potential venues; if your event is too close to a major holiday; or if it's in the month of June because it is a popular time for weddings.

### Putting "Butts in Chairs"

Crude or not, that's the slang those of us who put on live events use for boosting attendance. The entire name of the live event game is "butts in chairs." You can't sell them if they are not in the room! All of the elements of platform building covered in this book will help you get those butts in your chairs.

## THE WONDERFUL WORLD OF WEBINARS

Amy Porterfield changed my life. Not only is Amy the premier provider of webinar training, but her system works astonishingly well. It would be a disservice to you to tell you how to do webinars because everything I know that works came from her, although we've never spoken. I had done more than 300 webinars before I stumbled across her course at Profitable Webinars (http://bit.ly/ProfitableWebinars) and within a month of taking it, I earned more money than I had in all my previous webinars put together. This woman is a genius!

Webinars allow you to carefully craft your best content, market it, and deliver it to a very specific group of avatars. They allow you to serve people at the highest level. You earn money from them in one of three ways: you can charge for "tickets" to the webinar; you can sell a product or service during it (Amy's program explains how to find the right balance between serving and selling); or you can use webinars as freemiums or premiums.

When I give webinars specifically for authors or speakers, I am trying to get people to implement what I'm teaching so that we can eventually represent them and make a profit off their talent when their book or speech sells to a publisher or a meeting planner (see www.KellerMedia.com/webinars). What reasons would drive you to do webinars?

Most webinars are 30, 60, or 90 minutes in length. They are most often delivered with a PowerPoint presentation while using a service like GoToMeeting.com. The audience only sees your screen, not you. There's almost no cost in doing webinars, which makes them a great way to test your content's appeal to live people. Here are five tips I've learned that Amy does NOT teach:

1. Drink a big glass of room temperature water before you begin and keep another one near your desk, but try not to stop to sip. You're the whole show!
2. Take six or more deep, slow breaths before you hit "Start Broadcast."
3. Use polls to keep people engaged. It heightens your WIFM appeal.
4. Have a pen and paper handy to write down the first names of people who show up—it will help you to keep the audience engaged when you call them out by name during the program.
5. Put a brand new battery into your microphone before you plug it into your computer before you begin—and always use a microphone. (See Chapter 11, "Recording Sensational Audio" and recall my "frying eggs" experience without one.)

A friend took Amy's course a few months after hearing me rave about it. He put no soul in his slides or his marketing; he was not enthusiastic or confident in his subject matter, although in real life he is an undisputed expert; and he tried to sell a $5,750 product to people who had no idea who he was even after listening to his stilted 60-minute program. When it failed, he gave up. If you are a natural teacher, warm, personable, friendly, passionate, and good at sales, it may take you a few "practice" live webinars to get profitable, but Amy's program works miracles if you apply it. Here's the link again to find out more about it: http://bit.ly/ProfitableWebinars.

## WHEN TO START PROMOTING YOUR EVENT

The time to start promoting for a multi-day event or an event that most people will have to travel to is six months in advance. The time to start promoting a local event that you plan to sell tickets to is three months in advance. The time to start promoting a free live event is two months in advance. The majority of registrations will always come in during the last few days.

Here are a few extra promotional strategies to alert people to your live events (or webinars, for that matter!):

- Put a hyperlink and a call-to-action phrase in your email signature and instruct all your staff to do the same.
- Put a special announcement form in every bag or box you ship to or hand to your customers.
- Mail a hand-addressed "wedding invitation" style invite to every client or prospect in the geographic radius—a nice quality paper and a shiny metallic seal is a guaranteed 100 percent open rate!
- Put a banner ad on your website and any other related sites.
- Put a pop-up invite box on your website.
- Offer a free (something) to those who attend live.
- Hold a pre-event, also called a "feeder" event. When I was sponsoring a lot of multi-day expensive workshops for authors and speakers, I would do between three and six free feeder events in California and sometimes Arizona to prompt people to attend my costly live event in Los Angeles. Depending on your topic, you may be able to get other places to give you a free feeder event, complete with an audience. For example, local business clubs, charity groups, library talks, etc.
- Buy a few months of ads on the back of grocery store register tapes or display ads on the carts themselves (depending on the nature of your event, of course!).
- Ask other companies to sponsor your event, mail announcements about it to their compatible customers, or let you hang signs in their windows, especially if it's free and useful to their people.
- Stick a flier on local bulletin boards.
- Put it in the calendar section of your local newspapers (this only works if the event is free).
- Ask the community college and library to sponsor it or to host a few feeder events.

Follow these tips and you'll get lots of warm chairs!

# Chapter 22

# How to Get Paid to Give Speeches

What if you don't want to do the work of hosting your own events? Or you do not want the risk? Maybe you even want someone to pay you up front to speak to their audience, or perhaps you even want to make that a primary revenue stream for your business.

For instance, do you think Dr. Oz makes more money as a doctor or as a celebrity television host and speaker? Do you think most people do TED or TEDx talks (which are never paid) just for fun, or do you think they do it to grow their businesses, pitch or preach their message, or gain notoriety?

The glamour of being paid to share what you know from the stage cannot be overstated. Imagine an audience jumping to their feet and bursting into applause as you say your last few words!

You walk off the stage and a queue of people is already forming. They want to tell you how wonderful you were and how much you changed their lives. The meeting planner—the person who arranged for you to be hired for this event—is beaming at you from the bottom of the steps. She slips you an envelope, gushing over your incredible performance. Inside, there is a check for thousands of dollars. It's all yours, in appreciation for the knowledge you just shared in such a compelling, engaging, and clear manner.

When you get back to your hotel room, you check your calendar to see where you'll be speaking next week. Los Angeles! Perfect! You've got friends to hang out with there. You flop backwards onto the comfy mattress. Life is good.

If that's not your reality yet, read on.

## THE FIRST THREE STEPS

### Step One: Pick the Right Topic

Often, people want to get paid to speak on their favorite subject, not their smartest topic. Many people pitch me on how they overcame their abusive childhood, what they learned from their divorce, or how they almost took their company public—in the 1980s.

Without a lot of work, topics like those are unlikely to generate success. I define success as a speaker as the option to shrug off your job and/or triple your income within two years, like some of my clients and students have done.

The meetings industry is worth over a billion dollars. Of the money dedicated to hiring speakers, 85 percent is paid to those whose content is valuable and relevant to business audiences. Corporations hire speakers whom they believe will help them make more money.

To enter the speaking industry, or if you are getting off to a wobbly start, here are three tips to help you redirect some of that money into your pocket. To choose the right topic, bravely put your speech idea through this series of questions:

1. *Will a company make more money (have a happier staff, less turnover, sell more widgets, etc.) if they apply what I teach?* Can I prove it empirically?
2. *Am I really qualified to teach this?* There is more competition for that stage time than ever before. A person who tells me, "I was the salesman of the month three times at the Lexus dealership in my town" has a longer road to success than someone who says, "I am/was the highest grossing salesperson in the history of Lexus."
3. *Am I passionate enough about this topic to succeed?* I recommend to my clients and students that they plan to stay focused on the topic of their book and/or speech for two to five years. That means not just giving speeches, but continuously studying all the new, fresh content related to your topic. If you are already bored, it is the wrong topic. Your audience members should never know more than you do. You cannot rest on your laurels.

### Step Two: Look Before You Leap

Most people get starry-eyed when they talk to me about their future as speakers. They picture themselves becoming like Tony Robbins, with thousands of cheering fans and limos whisking them to events.

The reality even for the highest paid speakers is that you will spend way more time alone in hotel rooms; in long security lines at the airport; and in the back of cars than you will on the platform. Your primary task is transporting goods—and you are the goods. You are the product. It is yourself you are selling.

Speeches are usually between 45 and 90 minutes long. Most speakers invest two days of travel for that much time on stage.

Most mid-level speakers do about 20 engagements per year at an average fee of $5,000. That comes out to $100,000 per year. I train people who are still below that mid-level, and many of them have not thought through what it actually means to do 20 engagements a year. You can start training by visiting www.KellerMedia.com/webinars to take my free webinar "How to Get Paid to Give Speeches."

### Step Three: Do You Have "Platform" Skills?

"Platform skills" are industry jargon for how good you are on the platform. Are you authentic, likable, and interesting? Can you think on your feet? Are you resourceful? With good platform skills, your name will start to spread and speaking engagements will begin coming toward you. Take an improve class, sign up for community theatre, take voice or singing lessons. Train yourself for success.

I've been working with and for speakers since 1995, and I have yet to meet a new speaker who did not regale me with stories of how great he or she is on the platform. Ironically, I also work with many of the highest-paid speakers in the country, and every single one of them has told me about the acting coach they just hired, the movement coach, the voice coach, on and on. It is a business where success comes from constantly honing your craft.

Experienced speakers know that when you do a great job, word gets around. People talk about you behind your back—and say good things! The best speakers are always learning how to deliver their content better and how to market themselves better because they know continual improvement is the straight path to success. Boldly explore these three tips. They will determine your success velocity as a speaker.

## THE STEP-BY-STEP SPEAKER SELF-PROMOTION PLAN

1. Choose no more than three topics, all of which are of direct benefit to businesses, all loosely related. Businesses are where the money is in the speaking industry. If your topics are wildly divergent, e.g., "Customer Service, Positive Thinking, and Coping with Change," you sound like a Jack (or Jill) of all Trades, master of none.
2. Research the top 10 to 15 speakers who are already doing your topic. How are you different, deeper, more interesting, and more valuable to an audience?

3. Test and retest your proposed content via social media. If that proves that the general public likes what you say and how you say it, it will succeed as a speech topic. If they do not, you won't. Procter & Gamble doesn't release a new product without R&D (research and development) and market testing—neither should you!

4. Build a compelling, high-end website (check out www.PrimeConcepts.com for excellent speaker web design services). You need to invest in looking like a superstar if you want to get booked for money. The competition is fierce! People who have their wife's brother build their website after work are going to find they wasted time. This is an appearance-based business.

5. Leap onto the scene. Do not crawl! Write lots of blogs and articles; build a YouTube channel with branded, rich content; relentlessly introduce innovative, fresh solutions; comment publicly on new developments in your topic/industry. Be everywhere, all at once.

6. Identify and promote your availability directly to meeting planners.

7. Be professional, courteous, and diligent. When you get a meeting planner on the phone, have a clean, tight, benefits-laden pitch prepared.

Commit to pitching yourself to between 5 and 20 meeting planners every weekday for a few months before you get your first bite. In the beginning, it is "dialing for dollars." Of course, how you target meeting planners, get their contact information, and prepare to reach out to them in the most successful way possible is crucial.

Collect video of yourself speaking every time you get the chance, even if it is someone with a smartphone. Use it to improve. When you have at least five good clips, hire a professional to edit it into a dynamic speaker demo reel. (It's hard to get booked before you have one!)

Do a great job at every gig, even if it is the local nursing home. Be brilliant on the platform and professional, courteous, and charming off of it. Turn every meeting planner into a business friend so she will recommend you to peers. Marketing gets easier for speakers dedicated to self-improvement, who grow their content knowledge, improve their delivery style, and enhance their marketing strategies.

It is the daunting task of preparing the marketing materials and pitching yourself that imperils the success of most would-be speakers. If it were easy, everyone would do it. If you want this, it is a glamorous, interesting way to make a good living—and leave your mark on the world.

Marketing is the single most important task any speaker performs. This whole book is about platform, and while speaking is a way to build platform, you also need to have a platform to begin. (Sort of like when you were 16 and looking for your first job, right?) In the beginning, you will be your own marketing department.

Seeing as you are the person most passionate about selling your speeches, and you have the most to gain, that's not all bad, even if you hate selling! In my speaker training webinars and courses, I teach people how to get to that first $100,000 level. Next is an abridged version of the success strategy.

## HOW TO SELL FROM THE PLATFORM

There's an art and a science to selling from the platform. I've done private training for speakers on this topic for years. This is a wholly different process than selling one-to-one, selling online, or in a situation where someone came with the expectation of being a buyer, like when "selling" someone a new car.

Whether or not you charged for the ticket, you are likely doing your event to get people to buy something from you. Perhaps you want them to buy at the event or down the road. If you are speaking at someone else's event, most meeting planners (the people who hire speakers) insist that speakers do not sell from the platform (stage) because they don't want their audience to be treated like a room full of prospects.

There are ways to do it subtly, and effectively, so that the people in the audience do not even realize they are being sold to. Even the meeting planner will not notice if you do it properly.

The essential principles are these:

- People buy from people they like and trust—and you will never have them like and trust you more than they do when you are on stage in front of them. Use this precious time wisely.
- People buy based on unconscious commands delivered in auditory, visual, and kinesthetic ways.
- A sales "pitch" that works from the platform should sound like a friendly suggestion.
- People buy what they want, not what they need.
- Objections about price are most easily overcome from the authority of the stage.
- The more engagement and connection you create with the audience as individuals, the more you will sell—every time.
- Sales pitches get tuned out. "Happily Ever After" stories about your satisfied customers make people cozy up.
- People think in pictures. Help them see on a screen or in their mind's eye the picture of what they or their life will look like when they achieve the result you are promising with your product or service. Make them feel it, make it seem real.
- Think big, act bigger—look like someone who successfully sells what you're selling if you want to sell more of it (e.g., wear a ridiculously expensive tie and a lab

coat when you speak if you're selling personal genomic profiling; wear a designer suit and shoes while presenting).

- People like to be led. Emblazon the path, and they will walk down it at your suggestion. This is primal and applies to people of all IQ levels, socioeconomic levels, and occupations.

Just think through the ways you can apply these simple tips and you will already be in the 10 percent of those who are successful selling from the platform.

Go to any Anthony Robbins, Perry Marshall, or Dan Kennedy live event. Each are masters of platform selling in their own unique ways. Take notes on their styles, which are unique on the outside but quite similar on the inside. For good measure, go to the biggest multi-level marketing conference you can find. (Just be sure to hold onto your wallet!)

The professional speakers I see making the most money are those who look on their speaking as a major career path and who invest in learning, growing, and improving themselves and their marketing materials all the time. Just because you are fluent in your native language, have a desire to say something, and can make people laugh or cry, you are not necessarily ready to become a speaker. About 80 percent of the success is in marketing and 20 percent is in the content and delivery of your skills. The foregoing was just a taste of the industry so that you can decide if further study will help you grow your platform and live your dreams.

# Chapter 23

# Write a Book

Yep, I saved the best for last. I've represented more than 1,500 deals around the world, including 17 *New York Times* bestsellers and nine international bestsellers. Naturally, I've seen what a book can do for a "regular" person's platform. *Hint*: blow the lid off it!

I've consulted thousands of people on how to build a platform to sell more books, build a business around it, and to create a sustainable platform that will attract a major New York publisher before the book can be sold for a lot of money. In fact, this expertise is where the knowledge presented in this book began. Platform before, during, and after a book is critical to its success.

Popular culture has made the idea of authorship a romantic act. One invests heart and soul into the work, labors over every word, ideally wearing a tweed jacket with suede elbow patches. But if no one reads your book, it will not really matter what you wore while typing it! Platform is how you attract readers, and writing a book is part of how you can build your platform.

For some people, writing a book (or having one written in your name by a ghostwriter) is going to be the best platform building tool you have ever seen.

## FOR NOVELISTS ONLY

If you are one of the millions who only want to write the Great American Novel one day, this section will not help you achieve that goal. Feel free to skip it. This is for people who want to write a nonfiction book to build their business platform. The answers I am listening for are:

- To grow my business
- To bring in more customers, clients, or patients
- To establish my expertise in my subject area
- To launch or grow my speaking business
- To build my brand
- To foment massive social change
- To raise awareness of _____ (fill in the blank)

These are things a book can and truly should do. In my popular live webinar "Use Your Book to Build Your Business," I teach authors a few simple strategies to plot out the path to success. It starts, of course, with the topic you choose and how you prefer to present it, and it culminates in you reaping the benefits.

I have been a literary agent selling nonfiction books to top publishers around the world for almost 30 years. In that time, I have seen people who track their success from the day their first book was published. But on the flip side, I have also met people who claim their self-published book was one of the most expensive, unsuccessful, and time-consuming mistakes in their careers.

## THE FIRST QUESTION

If you came to me for potential representation, this is the first question I would ask you: Why do you want to be published? If your answer to my question is, "Everyone tells me I should" or "I want to become a full-time author," our conversation will be short. There is not much I can do to help someone who is not really motivated to get published or who does not want to make the book successful for reasons other than to earn royalties.

## STATE OF THE UNION

The mere state of being published will not achieve much. About 500,000 books are published and self-published annually in the United States. According to publishing industry research conducted by R.R. Bowker, only 17 percent of American households buy even one book in a given year, and not everybody will read the kind of book you want to write. If all you want is to get printed, you can write a check for a few thousand dollars to many of the subsidy publishers cropping up all over the country and let them tell you how wonderful your idea is. But if you want a book that will be done properly,

## TASTE TESTING YOUR BOOK

When I first proposed the book you are reading to my editor Jennifer Dorsey at Entrepreneur Press, I wanted to write exclusively about platform building for authors, speakers, and their ilk. This is a topic on which I am an indisputable expert. Jennifer flipped my idea on its head. She and I know that most people who want to become authors and speakers actually want that success to generate something for their own business, whether they are the CEO of a publicly-traded company or a small, one-person firm. We have worked with many people all across that spectrum. So she suggested I expand it to encompass everyone who is trying to build a platform, since it entails the same strategies. I had not considered that, but it was a better idea than my original one, and I seized upon it with the intent that I could help so many more people.

Sometimes, when authors come to me, I see something bigger for them, too. It grieves me when they resist. One of the things I look for in prospective clients is that they be flexible in pursuit of publication. Looking at something from a different perspective can make you see things in a whole new light. Should you get rebuffed by agents for your book idea (or not get adequate numbers of bookings for your speeches), seek out and heed good advice from those who have a qualified perspective.

One of the great things that happens when you are actively building your platform is that the marketplace responds to you. The avatars for your business are the avatars for your book. When you can show me that you have established a platform in your subject matter and now you want to parlay that into a hefty book contract, I can do it because your very success at platform building has taste-tested your topic. We know the public likes you and will buy your book. Since publishers are in business, and all business is in business to make a profit, you come with a ready-made marketing plan. That makes you desirable to publishers, and therefore to literary agents.

with a well-regarded publisher, so that it generates media, prestige, and respect, then the points in this chapter will be useful for you.

So how do you write a book to grow your business? What kind of book should you write? How should you publish it? What should you do to make the most of it once it is released?

## DO A LITTLE RESEARCH BEFORE YOU WRITE

Even if you intend to hire a ghostwriter to prepare the book proposal (the document agents use to sell nonfiction books to publishers) or to write your whole book manuscript, you should have a fairly clear picture of what you've got to add to the world that is New, Different, Better, or offers your readers something More (NDBM).

This means, at the very least, getting yourself into a bookstore or looking online and searching out books as close to your proposed topic as you can find. Buy them, read them, and figure out what you've got to say that is NDBM.

## THE PLANNING PHASE

When my daughter Sophie was about 10, she and her best girlfriend Taylor decided to build a tree house in my yard. They scavenged bits of a few 2 x 4s, got three nails, and borrowed a hammer. They started building.

It was never completed.

If you want to build a house, you would start with an architectural plan or at least an idea of what you want your house to look like, then assemble the materials before you began.

Why would writing a book be any different?

When you know what result you want from authorship, you can engineer a book that will get you there. I consult people all the time on this subject (if you are interested in my service, go to www.KellerMedia.com/rent) and go through this process for free with my clients. If you don't know where you are going, how will you know when you get there?

If you want to use the book to attract customers, what is the subject they are least informed about? What questions are you asked most frequently? What do they care about? What do they need to know before they work with you and your company? Sketch out four to six general ideas.

Once you have these general ideas, test them before a group of strangers. Your friends, parents, and employees are likely to tell you your work is great. Maybe even your spouse will compliment you. Unfortunately, their opinions are meaningless. They are not your target customers, and they presumably already like you and may not want to hurt your feelings.

## A NOTE TO THE WISE

If English is not your first language and you aren't 100 percent fluent, or if you know you make grammar and spelling errors just like you did in school way back when, hire an editor before you publish articles, blogs, ebooks, or books. This will save you embarrassment. You can hire inexpensive help from an English major from the local university or find someone on www.Craigslist.org, www.MediaBistro.com, or www.UpWork.com.

Instead, use your social media to test strangers' reactions to your content. Write a few blog posts on each idea. Do people engage with them? Do they like your Facebook page, comment on your LinkedIn blog, retweet your tweets? If you have been building your platform as you have been reading this book, you should have at least a few hundred people who are paying attention to you and your messaging by now. What do these people do when you post this content? They are the canaries in your mine. If they do not drop dead, you are doing fine.

Once you know your content has appeal to complete strangers who may or may not be prospects for your business, you have two choices: create an entire book or take an interim step.

See Chapter 9 for more information about creating and promoting a simple ebook to triple check your book's probability of generating success. You may find that is all you need to do and that a whole book is not necessary to achieve your aims.

## READY TO WRITE?

Once you know what your public wants and, in theory, will buy, it is time to make some decisions. Will you pursue a traditional publisher who pays you something for the right to publish your book and has a built-in series of checks and balances to help you create a successful book, or will you choose to self-publish and take all the risks and any potential benefits for yourself? See Figure 23–1, page 158 for a quiz that will help you decide.

Whether you create a book with a traditional publisher, a self-published book that you try to sell to strangers, or an ebook, putting your knowledge in written format will likely trigger a lot of ideas in your head. Can some of the information from your book be turned into scripts for videos? Content for blogs? A training program delivered live or online? The very process of writing a book may open your mind to a world of platform-building possibilities.

---

## Self-Publish or Traditional Publisher?

| | |
|---|---|
| 1. Do you want to pay someone to print your words? | ❏ True    ❏ False |
| 2. Do you want someone to pay you for the honor of publishing your book? | ❏ True    ❏ False |
| 3. Do you want a bunch of books in boxes in your garage? | ❏ True    ❏ False |
| 4. Do you want help editing, distributing, and promoting your book? | ❏ True    ❏ False |
| 5. Do you want to do most of the work yourself? | ❏ True    ❏ False |
| 6. Do you want esteem and credibility from becoming an author? | ❏ True    ❏ False |

*Answer key*: If you answered True to mostly odd-numbered pages, you should self-publish. If you answered True to mostly even numbered pages, you should do what it takes to attract a traditional publisher.

FIGURE 23–1. Self-Publish or Traditional Publisher Quiz

## HOW TO MAKE A BOOK MAKE YOU MONEY: 10 OUT OF 10,000 WAYS

It's lovely to get published. It may impress your friends and make your mom proud when she shows it off to all her friends at church or the senior center. But a book is a strategic, brand building business tool in my world.

Here are ten things authors under my supervision often do with their books to make money:

1. They use them as a textbook the consumer must buy when enrolling in their online training program.
2. They use them as lead-generating, door-opening tools with C-level executives for whom they wish to speak, train or consult.
3. They use the books to get media attention and then plaster those media clips or logos all over their business websites.
4. They take the overrun of the covers of their book (easy to get if ordered in advance from the printer or the publisher) and use them as innovative, unusual post cards to send to key prospects.

## HOW TO WRITE A GOOD NONFICTION BOOK PROPOSAL

A book proposal is the tool all literary agents must use to sell any non-fiction book to any publisher. A book proposal is to publishers what a business plan is to a venture capitalist—and for the same reason (you are trying to get a stranger to invest money in your idea).

There are six basic parts to a nonfiction book proposal:

1. *Overview*—where you talk about the big picture.
2. *Author's Bio*—where you show us how who you are is related to what you want to write, and make it clear that you're going to build your platform (*Hint. Hint*: you're reading a book on platform building right now!) so that the book makes money for you, your publisher and most important of all, your loving and adoring agent. (OK, well . . .)
3. *Marketing Plan*—where you tout the effects your platform building campaign has had so far.
4. *Chapter Summaries*—where you show us you have enough interesting content to fill 50,000 to 65,000 words in a way that readers will be satisfied and empowered to achieve the promise of the book, e.g., "Lose 30 lbs. in 30 Days" or "Build Jets at Home for Fun and Profit."
5. *Competitive Analysis*—where you show us why the industry needs yet another book on this subject. Because Solomon was right, there isn't anything new under the sun.
6. *One to Two Sample Chapters*—where you prove you can write in a manner that does not indicate that you were raised by chimpanzees nor that the only other writing you've ever done is technical manuals for Japanese auto manufacturers.

    Usually this is about 40 to 60 pages long. Edit the whole thing 8 to 10 times and then start seeking agents. We're the gate keepers of the industry, and your first avatars.

You can find literary agents in countless directories all over the internet. Make sure you look for an agent who specifically states that they handle books like yours. For instance, my agency doesn't handle children's books, true crime, screenplays, or first person stories of recent encounters with aliens, fairies, deities, invisible people, long-dead celebrities . . . .

5. They use the book as a way into exclusive meetings and networking groups whether their ideal avatars lurk.

6. They use excerpts from their books to fill their blog quota for a year (check with your publisher for permission!).

7. They use the fact of authorship to grow a big local image of success.

8. They write industry-specific supplemental ebooks to get specialty consulting contracts in those industries, using the book's prestige and the ebook's depth of knowledge to get attention.

9. They chop the book into scripts for short videos on their branded YouTube channels and then sell the book and their business at the end of every video, mention the YouTube channel in the book (sometimes before it is even launched) and put the book's name and the YouTube channel's address on all their marketing materials and business cards.

10. They offer the book as a gift to anyone who takes an action, like buying their product, coming into the store on Tuesday between 10 and noon, or anyone who shows up in their booth at the trade show. In other words, it becomes a freemium or a premium for certain desired actions a prospect takes.

There are a billion other clever business strategies that can be built on your professionally published book. I gleefully spend the biggest chunk of my time talking about how my authors can implement these kinds of things given their stated goals for the book. To give yourself a head start, pay attention to what other authors around you are doing with their books and look for models you think are effective and that you would like to emulate.

## WHY DOES ONE BOOK SELL AND ANOTHER FAIL?

Every author imagines that magic will happen and their book will end up on the *New York Times* best seller list, selling millions of copies, translated all over the world and getting them on all the major talk shows relevant to the topic.

As an agent, I have a rather cynical perspective, reinforced by my industry's hard statistics.

A self-published book for an author who does not have a platform will sell—if the author is lucky—117 copies in its first year.

A properly published book released by a professional publisher of good repute—will sell an average of just 2,500 copies in the first year . . . unless the author has a platform.

Everybody needs a crusade to build their life around and here's mine: Your book is a tool. It is a tool you can use to achieve a specific aim, like building a brand or growing a business or making everyone know you're the smartest person in your field.

The more authors who understand that, the better.

You may be writing your book to save the world. That's nice. But from my side of the desk, you have just one responsibility as an author: To get that book past the cash register. When it leaves Barnes & Noble or Amazon puts it in a box and ships it off to some hermit living in Wyoming with his pet buffalo, you have no more responsibility. You can't control whether the hermit reads it with his one good remaining eye, or whether the customer sets it on the "Someday" shelf.

And since there are so many books published in the U.S. every year, the chances of your fabulous, beloved book actually beating the odds by Divine Fiat and making it to the surface in this tsunami of words is very small.

This book, this labor of love you've crafted and sweated over, should definitely improve the lives of the people who actually get around to reading it. Statistically, we know most people never even make it all the way through the third chapter. (By the way, thanks for reading these words this far in, if you did. Send an email to IReadIt@KellerMedia.com and we'll email you a prize—seriously!)

So since most people aren't likely to read it, and since more likely than not you aren't going to get on the *New York Times* list without either a lot of money or a lot of effort implementing every single strategy in this platform building book, there's just one person you need to be worried about making happy: You.

Your book is a window of opportunity that begins the day an agent signs you on. Smart, marketing-oriented literary agents can explain to you how to start profiting from the fact your book is sold, even before you get the first advance check from your publisher.

Use this window of opportunity to build the prestige, expand your brand, crown your career, set up your speaking, dominate your industry, and attract as many ideal customers as your company can manage to bring in.

That's the guarantee. That's what a book will do for you. No one yet has invented a better way for an average person to get all that benefit than writing a book, except maybe if you get your own nationally-syndicated television show. (Good luck with that!)

Seize this chance! If you have taken the effort to build your platform, and it's working—more and more people are being attracted—then your time to write a book is now, while you're hot and ascending.

This book started, as I said earlier, because of a conversation with my wonderful, intelligent editor Jennifer Dorsey at Entrepreneur Press. I told her how sad I feel for misdirected authors who haven't a clue about how to turn a book into a business growth tool. Whether you want to write a book and attract a reputable, significant publisher, or whether you want to expand your business so it fulfills your wildest dreams for it, platform is the launching point for your success.

# Chapter 24

# Creating a Sustainable Platform

You've gone to all this work to get a platform. It is growing and attracting more and more customers to you. You may have some great responses and posts to your blog, and some wonderful testimonials from pleased clients. You may have learned that people really like it when you explain how to do things in minute detail, or that they respond most to inspiring feature stories about your best clients.

What does all of these mean? How do you put it all together and capitalize on it going forward?

Remember pages ago, when you made your first editorial calendar? Remember when we talked about avatars and analytics? After six months or so of platform building, you need to assess the results you're getting again. What are people responding to? What have you learned from the data you have been compiling? Should you be doing more of something and less of something else? Is your money and energy being well-spent?

Make adjustments.

Sometimes, the excitement of it all tends to encourage us to pursue a strategy that isn't paying off. Be tough with yourself. If you want to do media or vlog or make videos as part of your hobby, recognize it as that. But put your daily focus on the parts that are working best for you.

This applies to the avatars, too. Is it time to spruce them up a little? Did you find out that it is not only women between 25 and 55 who are interested in your product or service, but it is specifically women between 30 and 45 who have masters degrees and earn more than $100,000 per year who bring you the most benefit? In Perry Marshall's book *80/20 Sales and Marketing* he talks about how only 20 percent of our promotion efforts are bringing in 80 percent of our profits. If you can reassign 80 percent of your marketing energy and budget toward that 20 percent, what will happen then?

Platform building is a continual process. Leading your business to the next level is something you will be doing for the rest of your business life.

The principles in this book not only work, they are evergreen. They will work for you while you are just getting started, and they will work for you (technology permitting) in a decade. The principles are always the same: Find the people who want what you've got and give it to them in the ways they want to receive it.

You want to do three things to round out your success: First is to effectively manage your time and resources based on what you're learning; second, capture testimonials from the people who are most enthusiastic about you and your business; and third, keep doing what works. This is how you create a sustainable platform.

## MANAGING YOUR TIME AND RESOURCES

You could spend a lot of money hiring a social media firm to handle all your social media stuff, but they are unlikely to care about your business as much as you do; to deeply know and understand your avatars' innermost yearnings; or to be as attentive on a daily basis to your business' progress.

Some of my clients over the years have booked a film studio, hired a makeup artist, a hair stylist, a wardrobe stylist, a cameraman or two, and a film editor for thousands of dollars without having first tested their message, their delivery style, or even really having a clear picture of how they are going to promote their online training program or if their video blog content is something their marketplace even desires. That's wasting time and money.

Another category of entrepreneurs is do-it-all, know-it-all worrywarts who decide to do every single thing themselves, right this minute. Without a plan, they fry themselves pretty quickly and have to stop their progress because they are going in too many directions at once; they have destroyed their health or family life; or they have run out of money.

The way for none of those bad things to happen to you is a combination of analytics plus time management.

As we discussed in the analytics chapter, you want to keep tabs on what results you are getting from the efforts you are making. You probably use broad analytics in your business right now. "It cost me $8,000 to stay in business this month, from office rent to salaries, and we made $9,250, which means we profited $1,250." That's analytics.

When it comes to marketing, though, many entrepreneurs freeze. They don't know which metrics matter, nor how to interpret results. If you throw in the lingo used by some expensive social media expert, your brain may explode and you might find yourself saying, "Uh-huh. Yes. Let's go for another 90-day contract" without actually knowing what worked and what didn't. I'm not knocking social media experts—I use them myself—but only after I know what I want and expect from their work, and I am certain we have agreed upon certain checks and balances in the system.

Here are some important analytics questions you can use to assess your progress now that you have some hard data:

- How much money did we spend to acquire each customer?
- What is the lifetime value of a customer?
- What hidden costs (e.g., your time, average closing ratio, or shrinkage) am I perhaps not counting to acquire that customer?
- If I deduct the acquisition cost from the amount of the sale, what percentage of ROI am I making per customer?
- Which of my marketing efforts is specifically creating the best results?
- Can I replicate my success?
- Can I delegate more of what works and maintain quality?
- How do I identify and delete my marketing failures?
- If I put more money into X instead of Y, what happens?
- Should I continue doing this or not?

Since there's no way to guess which of the many marketing ideas and platform-building strategies from this book you have implemented, it comes down to the basic metrics.

## HOW TO CALCULATE THE VALUE OF A TRANSACTION

Memorize this equation:

Sale price – (cost of goods + amortized labor + lead acquisition) = true profit

*Example*: Let's say you sell an hourly consulting program, like I do (www.KellerMedia.com/rent). I charge $350 per hour. On the surface, that looks like pure profit. But here are the hidden costs in delivering that consulting hour:

- The merchant fees paid to my payment processing service.
- The credit card fees, which vary from 3 to 5 percent depending on which card the customer uses.

- Fees for the software program in the cloud that I subscribe to that delivered the email(s) that encouraged that person to hire me as a consultant for one hour.
- The software program I use to manage my schedule and allow people to book without human interaction.
- A tiny fraction of the fees I pay for my domain name and my hosting company for my website, not to mention the original costs of setting up the website.
- The labor costs incurred by the fact that one out of three people who buy a consulting hour with me feels the need to communicate with my team before the consultation about some tidbit, like they want to change the time but haven't pressed the hyperlink that would allow them to do automatically, or they want to ask if I got something they emailed me to read prior to the event.
- The monthly charges for the toll-free number the customer will use to dial in, and my associated costs of the incoming call, which is at my expense.
- The cost of keeping the office running for the hour I will be on the phone with that customer (staff, electricity, rent, etc.).
- The cost of customer attraction if I advertised to get that person to consult with me. (I do not do this, except in the broadest possible sense of offering it on my website and in a few emails per year.)

Then there's the cost of me taking an hour from what may well be more profitable work, depending on what I am negotiating with a publisher or working on for my business or a client that day.

I am a big believer in over-delivering, so the calls often go a little longer and/or I send the consulting client documents or materials afterward that will help him or her achieve their goals. These have their own production costs and economic values. Those things technically deduct even more from that original sum.

Extrapolated to the furthest level, my consulting skills come from the almost 30 years I've been in the business, the hundreds of conferences I've attended and spoken at all over the world, and literally the tens of thousands of people I've helped in similar situations (authors, speakers, small-business owners, and startups). It is critically important that you look at all the obvious and hidden costs when doing the same calculations for yourself. Yet that's still not the whole story.

## THE CHIGGER EFFECT

The other hidden factor that bites entrepreneurs is like a chigger. Chiggers, which my beloved Missouri-living stepmom Rita calls "No-See-Ums," are hard-to-see blood sucking tiny bugs that burrow into human flesh and drink our blood. In customer acquisition,

## RECIPE FOR CHIGGER REPELLANT

1. Determine your conversion rate.
2. Observe your sales process—are there warning signs that are consistent among the chiggers? Is there a question they often ask or is there a pattern their behavior follows?
3. Define on paper the typical characteristics of a chigger—make a chigger avatar, even. (Eew!)
4. Test your theory to see if you are right—do chiggers ever convert into profitable clients?
5. Remove the chigger politely by decreasing or ceasing all communication. Communication and interaction is the life blood chiggers seek.

the chiggers in your business do the same thing and have the same annoyance factor, and they can just as easily be overlooked until it is too late.

The Chigger Effect is when you end up allocating way more time than necessary to blood-sucking people who insidiously drain energy or resources. In sales, it's called your conversion percentage. How many people do you need to deal with in order to make a sale? How many of them are just blood suckers? "Tire kickers" or "Looky-loos"? What about the people who just want to talk but never buy?

You need a system for disqualifying your prospects. Jacques Werth's literally life-changing book, *High Probability Selling*, will help you create this system.

## WAYS TO IMPROVE YOUR CONVERSION RATE

When I worked in lots of telemarketing "boiler rooms" as a teenager, most sales people figured out the conversion rate pretty quickly, and the ambitious among us immediately set about trying to improve on it. If the average salesperson made 42 cold calls before making a sale (not unusual) then the smartest ones would always want to figure out how to get that down to 38. Or 29. Or 22 . . .

There are always ways if you search for them.

Your role is the same. One important component of your successful marketing campaign will be if you can face the facts about the obvious and not-so-obvious costs of customer acquisition, and then see if you can beat your own conversion rate. You can increase your conversion rate now and in the future with strategies like these:

- Direct your marketing to a more targeted, well-defined and better list of prospects—review and refine your avatars.
- Make your offer more compelling with add-ons and bonuses that have a high perceived value but that cost you little or nothing (reread Chapter 19 on sponsorship for ideas).
- Improve the quality, authenticity, warmth, sincerity, and compassion you display in your marketing communications.
- Increase the level of personal touch you give each customer, even if it is a one-off transaction like someone buying a can of soda from your convenience store.
- Explore creative ways to noticeably improve the customer experience.

One reason chain stores are taking over this country, and slowly European ones, is because of the standardization. A franchisor develops a successful system, sets a specific standard, inspects to make sure it is upheld, and the customer is assured of a relatively similar positive experience at that chain no matter where they find it in the world.

What experience is your customer having from the moment they first encounter your business?

Jeff Hayzlett, CEO of C-Suite Network, a large and growing business community, says, "When your customers or people that you could potentially do business with see you walk into the room, they see the business. When they see the business, they see you. There is no differentiation between you and your business when it comes to selling the business.

"Everything they touch, feel, see, or get to know about the business should be reflective of what you want it to look like and represent. A brand is nothing but a promise delivered. [You have to ask yourself] 'What am I delivering?' and then you should deliver on that promise. If you want to charge more money for your product, then look rich and deliver a rich experience . . . the service or value that you deliver to me [as a customer] is reflective of the price that I want to pay you."

When your marketing message, your image, your team, your interaction with your customers all say, "YES! We can help you achieve your goals. We can give you what you want at a fair price," then you are doing more to increase the revenue per customer and lower your conversion costs.

When I first began my transition from selling screenplays to selling only books, I went to countless writers' conferences and listened to anyone who wanted to tell me their idea for a book. Then I sold a lot of books for a lot of people, and built a reputation for excellence. A large number of my clients end up with best-selling books, lucrative speaking or consulting careers, and growing businesses, in whole or in part, because they worked with Keller Media, Inc.

After a decade or so, I decided not to advertise anymore. I don't go to writers' conferences. I don't even personally evaluate the books we are offered unless the project came by straight referral from an existing client, a colleague, or a highly placed peer. So my customer acquisition cost has gone down to just about zero.

Depending on the type of product or service you sell, this can be possible for you, too. As you get better at using your platform, you will quickly attract more and/or better quality leads. When you do a good job for them, word will spread.

Your conversion rate goes up and your customer acquisition costs go down when your platform improves enough to attract the right leads in the easiest way possible, and you ensure customers have an excellent experience.

Now your platform is your launch pad to the moon! You've really got the system working, growing, and generating lots of happy customers. That's great! You want to shout about your success from the rooftops. But that kind of looks a little like bragging, doesn't it? What kind of credibility do you really have if you walk around repeating the cheerleading chant my team and I used to use to try to salvage the morale of our always-losing team: "We're number one! Can't be number two! And we're gonna beat the whooopeee outta you!"

Yeah. Didn't work for our pathetic church basketball team, either. Your customers may not find it all that convincing either, even if it is true. But if you could just get other people to say such nice things about you . . . read on to find out how!

# Chapter 25

# How to Get and Use Endorsements, Testimonials, Referrals, and Reviews

One of the most overlooked yet critically important benefits of building a rock-solid business that really serves its customers is that people like what you're doing. Maybe some of them might send you referrals. They might give you a testimonial. They might endorse something you're doing. They might give feedback on new products or services you're thinking of launching.

Or they might not.

If you are doing a good job, but you aren't getting the kind of support you need from your customers, there can only be one reason: You aren't asking for it.

The nervous real estate agent who brings a potted plant the week after her buyers move into a house she just closed and titters, "Please refer your friends and family to me if they are looking for a house" does herself no favors.

The beauty salon that doesn't capture the name, email address, phone number, birthdate, wedding anniversary, and the children's names and ages (and remembers to commemorate these dates) for every single client does itself no favors and will always be "accepting walk-ins."

The business consultant who assures himself that someday some CEO will be golfing with another CEO and his name will maybe come up is likely to be taking a side job to support his consulting business for a few years.

The author who waits until two weeks before the book is due and then tries to suddenly reach out to Richard Branson, Sheryl Sandberg, or Jeff Hayzlett for endorsements will have a lot of blank pages at the front of the book.

## FOUR KINDS OF FRIENDLY FOLKS

### Testimonial

A testimonial comes from someone who used your product or service who is willing to write or be on camera talking about how good it is, you are, your team is, or what marvelous results they got from it.

### Endorsement

An endorsement is when someone with a big reputation says or implies, "I like this product. You should use it." A celebrity endorsement that always makes me laugh at its memory is when Sarah Jessica Parker, the actress who at that time was starring in the TV show, *Sex and the City,* was promoting Garnier's hair coloring. I'd put a lot of money on my assumption that she never used that product in her life, any more than a real athlete would drink a sports drink loaded with chemicals, artificial sweeteners and food coloring. But those are endorsements. People say to themselves, "Oh! If Sarah Jessica Parker uses it, it must be wonderful! Maybe I can have hair like that, too!"

### Referral

A referral is when someone tells another person that they recommend your product or service, your book, or your music. It's a pretty big deal when someone gives you a referral. They are putting a part of their relationship with that person on the line, and they are entrusting their friend, acquaintance, client or colleague to you. At the very least, remember to thank someone for the referral, or even send a small, tasteful (or tasty) gift. Cash is always popular.

### Review

A review is when someone writes or videos a comment on a review site like OpenTable, Amazon, or RateMyProfessor—any third party site that allows independent people to comment on an experience, product, service, or person. In theory, these people are not plants, but honest customers who had a positive experience.

The restaurant that tells itself that OpenTable, TripAdvisor, or Yelp reviews don't matter is going to be competing against every other restaurant in town for the foreseeable future.

The number one misconception most people have about asking for these things is that they think they are asking for a favor. Actually, you are making a square trade. You just have to see it from another perspective.

## THE RECIPROCITY FACTOR AND ENDEARING ENDORSEMENTS

The majority of people love to be asked for their opinion. You may have taken surveys on websites. The next time you take one, pay attention. Why did you agree to give some company your time? You're either very pleased or very annoyed. Are you noticing avatar defining questions? Are there questions that if answered positively, subtly seem like a public testament to that company's virtues? Once humans assert something publicly, they are less inclined to back down from their stated position. I always doubt how much the company really cares what I think of them. People just love to voice their opinions; it's part of our nature. Ask a customer who likes your business to comment on it and it will likely bring the customer a smile just to have been asked.

### Ask and Thou Shalt Be Given

When dealing with people who have bigger reputations, they are certainly getting something out of the trade. When Mr. Big Shot author endorses Smaller Shot author's book, the title of his book(s) will be mentioned in conjunction with his endorsement. If the customer hasn't yet bought Mr. Big Shot's book, that is one more opportunity for her to see it, think about it, and perhaps buy it. Remember the adage "5 hits makes the sale"? You've just put Mr. Big Shot's book title in front of your avatars, who are likely to also be his.

When Michael Jordan endorses Nike, he's getting a very, very big check. It's not coming from the goodness of his heart. I have a client who hired a reasonably well-known, beautiful female actress to "interview" him about his product on an infomercial he made for himself. Her fee was 50 percent of his company's entire annual marketing budget! He told me that his investment paid off less than 90 days after it began airing in the non-peak slots in the secondary media markets! You may or may not choose to pay for the endorsements you obtain—it depends on your networking skills, the web you've built around yourself, your degree of separation, and what you might have to trade that could be useful to the person you'd like to have endorse you.

## TYPES OF TOUCHING TESTIMONIALS

A testimonial is when any person—famous or not—writes or video tapes a sincere compliment. Here are some examples:

"Joe, your pizza is the best I've ever eaten!"

—Susan Kritzer, your hometown

"I can only say that working with you saved my life. The day I met you, Elizabeth, I had been thinking that it would be better to end my life than to continue with [this problem], but now . . ."

—Chelsea P.

"This man is the best person I have ever met in my life. He helped me figure out the entire theory of relativity. Thanks, Jim."

—Einstein

Testimonials are incredibly easy to get and incredibly useful to you. A testimonial guides your prospect to think, "Hey! Other people like this product or service, book, song, or artwork. I likely won't be screwed over if I buy this or use this. I won't be a weirdo if I like this. I can trust this company to give me what they seem to be promising."

Be on the lookout for upgrading from a "regular person" to the best-known person you can get. Of course, some of the most touching, emotional, sincere, and authentic testimonials will always stay on my websites (see an example of an effective testimonial page here: www.KellerMedia.com/testimonials), because they express eloquently what I want my prospects to hear. The bigger the name or job title of the person giving you the testimonial, the more valuable it is for you.

Testimonials work because me telling you how brilliant I am at marketing is suspect, but when you see dozens and dozens of my speakers and authors making lovely comments, some of whose books you are likely to know about or even have read, then you can believe that I really do know what I'm talking about.

## ROBUST REFERRALS

A passive referral happens when John says to Scott, "I'm thinking of getting a Lexus like yours. Where did you buy it?" and Scott tells him "Oh, at Main Street Lexus on Third Street." That's passive because Scott was just standing there with his car keys when John approached him. Can't say no to that, but there's another way to get referrals that is much more proactive: Asking for and rewarding people for referring you.

Your thank you could be money, a percentage, an affiliate fee, services, products, a thank-you card, or gifts. It need not be lavish, but don't make it cheap, either.

You can have a policy that says: "We pay 10 percent for referrals" or you can just surprise people when they do it. Which do you think would have better results in your business? Decide, and then start asking for referrals boldly.

## REVELATORY REVIEWS

People trust reviews. They assume (sometimes incorrectly) that the reviewers are all unpaid people just like them who are making honest assessments. Just the proliferation of review sites online should alert you to the fact that reviews are super important.

I found my CPA on Yelp years ago. I told her how I found her the first day I met her, but it was years before she printed and framed little signs all around her office that say, "Like us? Yelp us!" with her logo on it.

Remember to go onto the primary review sites now and again to refute or make amends for the bad reviews, but even more important, to graciously and publicly thank anyone who has given you a good one. (And send them a little something—even just a physical card.)

Pay attention to reviews—the good and the bad. You can learn what you're doing right and wrong in your business. They are precious.

## BLUSHING FOR DOLLARS

"Oh," you may be thinking, "I don't want to ask for this kind of stuff. I'd be embarrassed." My retort: "Would you rather be embarrassed or broke?"

Testimonials, endorsements, reviews, and referrals help more people trust in your product or service. If you believe in your company, there's nothing better than to share the good news of what your happy customers are saying about you, so that new customers can be happy, too.

In fourth grade, I realized that all my friends' mothers cut their children's sandwiches diagonally, not simply in half as my mother did. I hinted. I sort of asked. I wondered. I worried. Was this a sign that I was less loved than my friends? I even told my mother that Cherie Ann's mother always cut her sandwiches diagonally, at the very moment she was holding the knife over my PB&J. She never got the message.

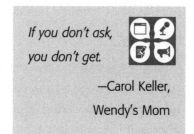

*If you don't ask, you don't get.*

—Carol Keller,
Wendy's Mom

Eventually, I screwed up my courage and point blank asked her to do this marvelous thing for me. I fumbled my request, wringing my hands. She looked at me kind of funny and said, "Sure." Beat. Beat. Then she gave me this life lesson: "If you don't ask, you don't get."

Please take my dear mother's words to heart, right here and now, as it pertains to you asking for referrals, reviews, endorsements, and testimonials.

## HOW TO ASK FOR WHAT YOU WANT

So how do you screw up your courage to ask for these things? And what do you do with them once you get them? And how can you use them?

Luckily, I've learned a lot about this topic since fourth grade.

- Every time someone compliments you, your business, your team, or your product, say, "Can you put that in writing?"
- Decide where you'd like them to put it in writing. The websites mentioned above, especially Yelp, strongly affect the traffic you get for small businesses in urban areas. If you don't know where you'd like reviews to appear, ask your new customers where they first heard about you and once you know, tell anyone who asks that that's where you want them to write the review.
- For many businesses, customers are attracted via a website. Get your happy customers to write you testimonials and give you signed releases allowing you to use them anywhere any time you want. (If you'd like a copy of the release form we use for this purpose, please go to www.KellerMedia.com/sample-release. We'll be glad to share it with you. Make certain to get it reviewed by your attorney, just to be on the safe side.)
- Slap those testimonials all over your marketing materials. All over your website. Heck, paint them on a sandwich board and walk up and down the street!
- You probably have been in a dry cleaning establishment that has pictures (faded, cheaply framed) of old celebrities, all of which are signed by the celebrity (allegedly) and often say, "Joe, thanks for the great service!" Well, I hate to blow your dry cleaner's cover, but you can buy those or even get them for free from most celebrities' PR offices. Why? Because it's marketing for the celebrity as much as it is for the dry cleaner. How much more useful is it for you to have testimonials, pictures, and even video clips of yourself with big shots?

My friend Mark Victor Hanson, co-author of the *Chicken Soup for the Soul* series, told me once that he has a photo taken with every single important person or celebrity he meets. And that was before he was one! The walls of his office are overflowing with photos of him with just about everyone on the planet and off it who has a recognizable face. You probably won't also get to meet Neil Armstrong, the first man on the moon (especially since he is now dead), but you may someday rub shoulders with the mayor in your town, or the CEO of the company you buy widgets from, or the CEO of some publicly traded company who is in the bathroom at the same time you are at a trade show, or even the local news anchor, or . . .

When you take a snap with these people, you immediately elevate yourself visually to their level, assuming you don't look inappropriately dressed. Frame that photo and put it on the wall where you customers can see it. Show off on Facebook.

There's a big framed shot of me with Dr. Phil right behind me on my office wall. It was taken minutes after he had me on his show to talk about (among other things) my book, *Secrets of Successful Negotiation*. That photo is not there so I can see it—I already know I was on his show (before he changed to the more Maury Povich style content). It's there so you can see it when I record a vlog or take a Skype call.

There are overt and subtle ways to promote yourself using testimonials, reviews, recommendations, endorsements, and even pictures. Using these as you get them will help your customers feel more confident in you, your team, your product, and your service. It will help them trust you—maybe even predispose them to liking you. Of course you remember: People do business with people they like and trust.

# Chapter 26

# Profiting Forward

In these pages, you've been exposed to enough marketing ideas, strategies, and principles to build your business to the exact level of success you desire. You have all the tools you need. You obviously have a commitment to success if you've read to this page.

But have you done anything yet?

Has this been another "shelf-help" book to which you say, "Oh, yeah. I'm going to do that someday, for certain"? But then someday never comes?

I hope not. One small step is better than no steps. Even a "good enough" blog, video, or ebook is better than a "not started" product. Yes, you've got an image to uphold. And yes, like I told my daughter a million times, "A job worth doing is worth doing well."

But if you don't start, you can't finish. If you don't get going, you won't get to the benefits. I didn't make this stuff up. It works if you work it, and it doesn't if you don't.

I am reminded of the old joke, "How do you eat an elephant?"

The answer: "One bite at a time!" (*Note*: I am not really recommending pachyderm parmigiana on your menu!)

But I'm sure by this point in your life, you have noticed that baby steps in the right direction eventually get you somewhere. In time, we all learned to walk, then run, then stride, skip, hop, leap, gallop—you get the point.

I have had the honor of consulting a lot of small business owners, some just starting out, some far down the road. One thing I know for sure is that those who boldly set out to do our own thing, work for ourselves—we are a special breed. We put our livelihoods and in some ways our lives on the line. We work harder and smarter. We fashion a company out of nothing but an idea. We bring an exceptional amount of courage, intelligence, and plain old guts to work every day.

Whether your business is selling a product or a service, or trying to make a living out of a creative product like a book or a song, you have shown exceptional faith. Faith in yourself, and faith that you will find the answers, the help, the support, and the guidance you need.

I hope you've found inspiration in these pages.

I believe owning a business is a glorious mission. Your business allows you to provide for your family, provide jobs for others so they can provide for theirs, create happy customers who are having some need or desire met, help support all your vendors, and give you a fantastic stage on which to fully exercise your talents and skills while you grow your character.

I trust that you will take the spark we've kindled together and grow your flame with it. Thank you for reading this book. If I can help you in any way, please connect with me via our website www.KellerMedia.com or call (800) 278-8706. And because "if you don't ask, you don't get it," please take a moment now to review this book on Amazon, Barnes & Noble, or your favorite retailer site.

May your business flourish, and your life overflow with an abundance of all good things.

# Resources and Links

## KELLER MEDIA LINKS, BONUSES, AND PROGRAMS

Wendy's site where you can find lots of cool stuff for authors, speakers, and small business owners: www.KellerMedia.com.

Where to discover your natural aptitudes and talents so you can build a great platform easily: www.KellerMedia.com/BizQuiz.

Free live webinars hosted by Wendy, stuffed with specific information: www.KellerMedia.com/Webinars.

Private hour of consulting with Wendy: http://KellerMedia.com/Rent.

List of all the sites we know that aggregate journalist's names and contact info: www.KellerMedia.com/Find-Media.

View a few sample Facebook public figure page banners: www.Facebook.com/KellerMediaInc AND www.Facebook.com/WendyKellerCompassionPage.

See some sample press releases so you have a template for writing yours: www.KellerMedia.com/Press-Release.

Get an example of a release for your testimonials: www.KellerMedia.com/Sample-Release.

See an example of a good testimonials page: www.KellerMedia.com/Testimonials.

Learn how to do a video blog: http://bit.ly/1r5nlly.

Pitch Keller Media on your nonfiction book: www.KellerMedia.com/query.

Hear Stephen Woessner's first podcast interview with Wendy:
www.OnwardNation.com/wendy-keller/.

See an example of a philanthropic website: www.WendyKeller.com.

## WENDY'S RECOMMENDED RESOURCES

This is my personal list of the best companies to work with for small businesspeople. I am sharing it to help you. Most of these are companies or people that I trust after sifting through their competitors during my almost 30 years in business; some were highly recommended by my clients or friends and I don't work with them personally. This is by no means a comprehensive list. You are responsible for your own decisions. *Caveat emptor.*

### Website-Related

Top website creation and online marketing company: www.PrimeConcepts.com.

Keller Media's fabulous, reliable hosting company: www.MediaTemple.net.

Best place to buy domain names: www.GoDaddy.com.

### Preferred Auto-Responder, Database Management, and CRM Providers

Companies that can handle your auto-responder and help you collect your prospects' email addresses:

- *www.ConstantContact.com* (free until you exceed a certain number)
- *www.InfusionSoft.com* (this is the number one company in the U.S. for marketing automation. Wendy has been their customer since June 2011. They are the premier provider—with prices to match.)
- *www.MailChimp.com* (free until you exceed a certain number)
- *www.SalesForce.com* (the world's leading CRM for sales management)

### People to Hire

Where to look for book writers, sound engineers, graphic designers, ghostwriters, copywriters, and other creative services:

- www.eLance.com

- www.ODesk.com

- www.Fiverr.com

- www.MediaBistro.com

- www.Craigslist.org (post or look in the "Gigs" section)

Where to look for virtual assistance:

- www.123Employee.com/platform

## Graphics Related

Where to get licensed images to use in your materials:

- www.Dreamstime.com

- www.GettyImages.com

- www.ShutterStock.com

Where to create images to use in your materials:

- www.Snappa.io

- www.Canva.com

- www.MyECoverMaker.com

- www.PlaceIt.net

## Marketing Training

Where to learn everything there is to know about doing great webinars:

- http://bit.ly/ProfitableWebinars

Where to host and how to promote your webinars:

- www.GoToWebinar.com

- www.LeadPages.net

- www.WebinarJam.com

## Video and Audio Related Resources

Where to buy equipment online:

- Amazon

- eBay

Where to upload your videos:

- www.Vimeo.com

Where to deliver/post your videos:

- www.YouTube.com

- www.Facebook.com

Where to get some decent teleprompter software:

- www.promptsmart.com

Where to get a great video editing program:

- www.Wondershare.net

Where to upload your audios:

- www.Libsyn.com

Where to sell your audios/podcasts:

- www.Stitcher.com

How to deliver your audios:

- iTunes

## General Stuff You'll Need

Best information on writing a sponsorship proposal:

- www.GetSponsoredFast.com

Audio file transcription service:

- www.Rev.com

Where to put big files so that your audio or graphics people can collect and return them to you easily:

- www.Dropbox.com

Where to have a great time in Arizona:

- www.ClownTownHealingFest.com

## MEET THE STARS!

Do you want to connect with one of the other experts mentioned in this book? There are so many! Here are super short bios and links to help you reach my world-class friends, clients, peers, and advisors.

**Laurie Allen**: Laurie is a top radio personality in the crazy-competitive Los Angeles market. She was one of the first women in the business, and if you ever hear her voice, you'll know why she was able to rise so quickly. To connect with Laurie, go here: www. gocountry105.com/programming/hosts/bios/?id=27 and tell her Wendy Keller referred you.

**Ryan Blane**: Ryan is considered one of the nation's leading authorities on the process of obtaining sponsorships. His method has worked for small businesses, artists, musicians, nonprofits, big businesses, authors, and more. If you'd like someone else to write you a check to promote your art, product, or service, connect with Ryan here: www. GetSponsoredFast.com and tell him Wendy Keller sent you.

**Geoff Colon**: As literary agents who specialize in nonfiction, we get offered a lot of projects every year by all kinds of people. But when Geoff Colon offered me the chance to consider representing his book, I immediately knew a big fish had just swum into my end of the pond. Geoff is a renowned marketing consultant, currently helping out at Microsoft. I can see why they retained his services. He blogs, teaches, speaks, and consults. His take on marketing is so refreshing it is called "disruptive." In fact, that's the title of his eye-opening book, *Disruptive Marketing: What Growth Hackers, Data Punks, and Other Hybrid Thinkers Can Teach Us About Navigating the New Normal*. If you want to revolutionize the way you attract customers, this is the book you'll want to buy. Go here to grab a copy: geoffreycolon.net.

**Dodinsky:** If you're a human being, chances are you suffer from the ups and downs of life. Dodinsky could be the remedy you need! Here are his two best websites, both perfect for you if you want a jolt of good cheer: www.facebook.com/Dodinsky and www.Facebook.com/PositiveOutlooks.

**Michael Glauser**: This man makes me wish I were just entering college again! Mike is a professor at the Jon M. Huntsman School of Business in Utah, and the author of *Main Street Entrepreneur: Build Your Dream Company Doing What You Love Where You Live*. (Yep, I'm his agent!) His warmth and wisdom are exceptional, and his approach to entrepreneurship incredibly inspiring.

**Jeffrey Hayzlett:** Jeff Hayzlett is a force of nature! He was a leader in the printing industry when I met him, just getting into paid public speaking. His career has been astronomical! Today, he is the CEO of the C-Suite Network (http:c-suitenetwork.com), which serves business people with content, information, advice, and live events. He is a top-level speaker, business consultant, and media personality in the business world, and author of three successful books (all of them represented by me!) www.Hayzlett.com. He's also one heck of a wonderful person!

**Perry Marshall:** Perry has one of the brightest marketing minds you'll ever meet. He's the author of many books (type his name in an Amazon search!). I especially love his book on Facebook advertising, which is the one that turned me into his ardent fan before I became his friend and agent. He directly influences the lives and destinies of many thousands of entrepreneurs worldwide with his revolutionary and practical content. Get yourself access at www.PerryMarshall.com and tell him Wendy sent you.

**Daven Michaels:** Think of the most positive-thinking person you know. Now multiply that by 20, and you've got the Energizer Bunny of Business, Daven Michaels. I've rarely had a conversation with him that didn't include the words, "We started another business and . . ." Usually, he'll go on to tell me how many customers it has attracted in just X months in business. And he's not exaggerating! Part of Daven's success is described in his *New York Times* best selling book *Outsource Smart*. (P.S.: This is the How To component Tim Ferriss left out of *The Four-Hour Work Week*.) But after watching him for years, the real secret to his unending, unfathomable success is this: he lives what he preaches! Daven really does have the best grasp of delegation of anyone I've ever seen at any business level. That could be because he owns one of the largest, fastest-growing and highly rated offshore outsourcing companies in the world: www.123Employee.com. If you're feeling buggered by the amount of work on your shoulders, they can help you with pretty much every platform strategy described in this book.

**Ronan Chris Murphy**: If your side dream is to be a world-class recording artist, you could do no better than to study with the world-class Ronan. We met at a coffee shop when I noticed he was also studying Italian. He now teaches sold-out recording boot camps in Italy, the U.S., and online. Go to www.recordingbootcamp.com/ to find out more.

**Amy Porterfield**: I've mentored dozens of women who are launching their own businesses, and I've met most of the women who run those "how women can start a business" seminars. Amy Porterfield is what most women in business hope to become: respected as the absolute leader in her field. Her course on webinars opened up a revenue stream for Keller Media that I didn't even really believe existed. Every marketing professional I know considers her products the gold standard for comprehensiveness, organization, clarity, and the ease of implementation. Check out Amy's best program by clicking here: http://bit.ly/ProfitableWebinars. It can change your life, as it did mine.

**Judy Robinett**: At the end of the day, business success comes down to who you know. And I'm glad to know and represent the irrepressible, brilliant networker, speaker, and author Judy Robinett. The first book I sold for her, *How to be a Power Connector: The 5+50+100 Rule for Turning Your Business Network into Profits* is the most comprehensive system for getting to know the people you most need to know to grow your business. Even for bookworms like me! Click here to get yourself a copy. If you can read just two business books this whole year (the one you're reading right now counts as one!), this is the other one to choose.

**Mitch Russo:** Imagine one day you were biking across CalTech and bumped into Einstein. Would you recognize him and his great contribution to society? Probably not. Posterity gave Einstein his gloss. Well, lucky for us all, I wasn't the first to recognize the jaw-dropping genius of Mitch Russo. Truly, one of the best-kept-secret business minds on the planet. You think that's fluff? His client list—if he reveals it to you—will make your head spin. He only advises companies very selectively these days, but at the very least, touch the hem of his garment here and watch your business be healed: http://www.invisibleorganization.com/

**Ford Saeks:** I knew Ford Saeks as a legend before I ever met him as a real live human. I've been in and around professional speakers since 1995, and I heard his name repeated with near-reverence. Ford is a unique combination—a brilliant small business strategist plus a business speaker—he runs the most impressive website development company I've ever encountered. I think I'm on my eighth website for Keller Media (and yes, of course Ford's company created my current ones). He's known as the go-to guy for speakers and authors seeking websites that sell speeches and/or books, and I know they work with a lot of people outside those industries, too. To check out Ford's genius, go to www.ProfitRichResults.com and to see some of the most stunning websites ever, go over to www.PrimeConcepts.com. Tell 'em Wendy Keller says hello.

**Stephen Woessner**: In the last 30 years in business, whenever I described my "ideal avatar" for the agency, I was describing people like Stephen Woessner! I said, "My ideal avatar is someone who is brilliant at what he or she does; has a track record of success; and understands that marketing is the foundation of selling anything." And the icing on the cake? He's still humble enough to enthusiastically take and implement advice from experts in fields other than his own. Stephen and I met when he invited me to be a guest expert on his podcast www.OnWardNation.com. That's one of America's fastest-growing business podcasts! Not only did I leap at the chance, I also recommended several of my biggest clients be interviewed by Stephen. But best of all, at the end of that first interview, I told him, "You should write a book!" Less than two months later, he'd done precisely what I instructed. The book was sold to an enthusiastic publisher and is titled *The Complete 20-Step Sales Generating Podcast System for Business Owners Who Want to Grow Revenue and Build a Nation of True Fans*. Stephen takes action and gets the job done. His core business is in digital marketing. (www.PredictiveROI.com), where his team helps businesses build impressive online impact quickly. Whenever I find myself starting to resist input from an expert in my personal or professional life, I always reflect on Stephen's example of responsiveness.

# Glossary

**Affiliate**: a person or company with whom one creates a mutually beneficial deal, such as one promoting the other's products or services for an agreed-upon percentage of the profits

**Avatar**: a composite persona reflecting the theoretical interests, demographics, and other data about a specific type of prospect or customer

**Blogging**: the act of writing an article or opinion piece intended to be delivered and read online

**Bonus**: something extra you give away to incentivize someone to take the desired action

**Control Group**: a research term that refers to the untampered with group of people, ads, or even animals against whom we can compare responses during marketing tests. Example: a new drug that is being tested using a control group means that the control group are the people who get the placebo, not the drug. This is to evaluate the effects that the new drug has on the people who end up taking it and how those effects differ from the normal behaviors/reactions of the control group.

**Conversion**: someone taking the action you desired them to take (*see Conversion Percentage*)

**Conversion Percentage**: the percentage of people who take the action you want them to take, whether that action is buying a product, clicking a link, or taking a free ebook. If 100 people see your ad, for example, and 10 of them take the desired action, then 10 percent is your conversion percentage.

**CRM**: Client Relationship Management software or service. Many CRMs include autoresponders; some excel at helping sales people interact with a prospect (Act! at www.Act.com and SalesForce at www.SalesForce.com); some are genius at helping you create outbound marketing campaigns (www.Infusionsoft.com); features vary widely among providers, and it is hard to change from one to another once you invest.

**CTA**: Call to action. When you say, "Click here" or "Call now" you are rendering a CTA—a direct command to take the action that will lead to the conversion you desire.

**Customer**: any person who has the good sense to give you money for your product or service.

**Demographics**: the physical data one collects about a customer or prospect. Demographics is where they live, how old they are, their income level, their zip code, their race, their education level, etc. (*see Psychographics*)

**eBook**: a book or book-like document that is delivered electronically to the customer, either by a distribution hub such as Amazon or by emailing a .PDF attachment.

**Freemium**: Any product or service that is intended to build a bond and/or stimulate a sense of obligation with a current or future customer. Usually, a freemium is delivered online in audio or print format, such as an informative MP4 or an ebook. (*See also Premium.*)

**Infographic**: an image designed to quickly and easily convey a large amount of information—Information plus Graphic.

**Infopreneur**: any individual who makes income from the sale of information in any format.

**ISBN**: an acronym for International System Book Numbering. The digits on a book that identify that particular book, its edition number, and its publisher to facilitate its retail distribution.

**Keyword**: a word used to direct people toward a specific online location. For example, if someone is looking for "locks," they might use the keywords "aluminum combination locks" or "Sentry padlocks" to find them.

**Lead**: the name and usually also the contact information (email, phone, or address) of any person whom you consider a prospect for your company.

**Lead Magnet**: any freemium, give-away, contest, bonus, premium, or other product or service used to attract leads to your business.

**Market Share**: how much of the available sales of a product or service in a region or industry are gathered by one company (ideally yours!).

**Meta-Tag**: a specific word, keyword, or phrase that is embedded into the coding of a website to help web crawlers and search engines identify your site and deliver it to anyone searching for those specific words or phrases. (These are not as important as they used to be, but some search engines still use them.)

**Metrics**: the data and numbers that result from analytics. Numbers you use to make a decision about how to spend your marketing resources.

**Non-Peak Slots**: a television industry reference for any opening in a station's schedule that occurs when few viewers are tuned in, for instance, between 3 and 4 A.M. These non-peak time slots are usually available for a pittance compared to what you would pay to place a show or infomercial when the majority of viewers are awake and active.

**Open Rate**: the percentage of people who open an email. For example, if you send an email to 2,000 people and 20 open it, you have a 1 percent open rate.

**Phoner**: slang for a radio interview done by phone or Skype, where the person being interviewed is not in the studio during the interview.

**Platform**: a large, growing group of people who like what you have to say or sell, in any media, for any reasons, at any time. (*See also Tribe.*)

**Point-of-Purchase**: any items, usually with high appeal and small cost, sold near the cash register in a store of any kind.

**Premium**: traditionally, a "gift with purchase." Any extra item or service used to incentivize a sale and only available to the customer once they give you money.

**Principle of One Thousand**: the unwritten rule that 1,000 people need to see any marketing piece before a clear determination can be made about its efficacy. It is not uncommon to use 500 as a fair test, but rarely fewer than that.

**Prospects**: the wonderful, lovely, darling people who are likely to give you money soon if you apply the principles in this book. (*See also Lead.*)

**Psychographics**: the intangible but useful data you can gather about a prospect that will enhance your ability to sort them and connect with them on their wave length. This is about how they think and see the world. For instance, whether they like horses, race cars, gardening, or imported green tea; their political leanings; religious point of view; and favorite color.

**Purchase Frequency**: a term for how often your customers purchase products like yours. For example, a new roof vs. a carton of milk entail widely different purchase frequencies.

**Quota**: the number or dollar value of sales assigned to an individual. Basically, how much the boss expects a salesperson to sell to "earn their keep" and help make a profit. If you are the only salesperson you employ, I believe you should set a quota for yourself daily, weekly, or monthly.

**Rate Card**: advertising industry jargon for the menu of ad sizes and types available for purchase in a publication.

**ROI**: the Return on Investment made. For example, if you spend $1,500 on a display ad and attract $2,000 in new sales, your ROI is $500 because you made an extra $500 you wouldn't have had if you hadn't spent the $1,500.

**RSS Feed**: the "RSS" stands for "Rich Site Summary." It is basically a method by which people can stay up-to-date with the most recent online content you publish. For example, those who subscribe to your RSS Feed will automatically be notified every time you publish a new article or blog post.

**Search Engine**: loosely, the system by which websites are sorted, their content identified and delivered to a user. Common search engines in the U.S. are Google, Bing, and Yahoo.

**Solopreneur**: an individual who works alone. May include someone who has only virtual support part-time. This is the fastest growing segment of the work force.

**Split Test**: the valuable and informative process of testing A against B, as in sending 500 people to Ad A with the blue background and 500 people to Ad B with the green background to determine whether your customers prefer blue or green.

**Sponsorship**: When a company or person donates money, time, or other valuable goods to another company or person for charitable or commercial purposes.

**Traffic**: all the people you can get to see your storefront, your website, your ad, anything you're trying to show them to lure them into doing business with you.

**Tribe**: the aggregate group of all your fans, in any location or format. People who like you and/or what you've got to sell. One uses platform building to increase the size of one's tribe.

**URL**: URL stands for "Uniform Resource Locator." It is the address of a web page, for example www.KellerMedia.com is my URL.

**USP**: unique selling proposition. This common term is used by marketers to mean what makes a person, business, brand, location, product, or service interesting, original, refreshing, and attractive to customers. "Unique" makes it easier to market and sell. In a world of almost-the-sames, "unique" is a loose term. Basically, focus on what you've got that is different.

**Venue**: where a gathering is held. Common venues are hotel meeting rooms, offices, and restaurants.

**Vlogging**: an amalgam of the words "video" and "blog," which is when a blog is delivered to consumers in video format (and perhaps simultaneously in print). Usually, the blog author reads the blog into a camera.

**Webmaster**: the valuable technical person in charge of building, maintaining, modifying, and monitoring websites. (Meet Keller Media's at www.PrimeConcepts.com.)

**WIFM**: the most important acronym you'll ever learn as a business person! Stands for "What's in it for me?" and it is said as a reminder to always think about everything you do and say to promote your business and sell your wares from the customer's perspective because that's all the customer is thinking about.

# Acknowledgments

A book is the physical manifestation of the knowledge on a particular topic someone has gained up to that point in time. It summarizes that author's perspective and expertise and shares it in a way that is intended to benefit the readers.

How can a lifetime of mentors, teachers, guides, professors, inspirations, heroes, failures, bad examples, mistakes, achievements, open doors, closed doors, and all the other hard-won factors that produce expertise be summarized? Just the list of names starting from birth would be longer than the book itself!

Naturally, I thank my parents Larry and Carol Keller for their love and support.

Others whose influence can be distinctly articulated in the contents of this book have been named within its pages. To every marketer who has influenced me in private conversations, and every marketing author whose book I've ever read or represented, thank you. To all the journalists I've worked beside or who have interviewed me, thank you.

To my colleague Megan Close, literary agent, for her consistent encouragement and gentle early editing, thank you.

As readers, you may never know how many people behind the scenes have been instrumental in bringing this information to your hands.

They deserve to take a bow. They are my publisher Jennifer Dorsey, and the marketing professional Vanessa Campos, both of Entrepreneur Media. Applause! Applause!

Jennifer, Vanessa, my terrific editors Karen Billipp, Michelle Martinez, and Valerie Cooper, and all their colleagues have given me this opportunity to codify and share with you how to build a platform that grows your business. In that joint effort, they are my sisters in helping you achieve your goals, build your business, expand your brand, and impact the world in the ways that are meaningful to you. It truly is all about you and your needs.

Thank you for picking up our book. It will be up to you to decide what you will do with this knowledge now. Your success is in your hands . . . literally.

# About the Author

Wendy Keller's company Keller Media, Inc. sells good books to good publishers and helps train authors and speakers to succeed.

Each author and speaker is considered a unique small business entity at Keller Media, with unique goals and a particular business strategy for obtaining them.

Personally, Wendy is passionate about marketing. She consults interesting businesses of many sizes and in varied industries to help them grow in efficient, effective ways.

Wendy speaks to audiences on all aspects of platform building, branding, publishing, and how to get paid to give speeches.

To discover how you and your company might benefit from working with Wendy or her team, go to www.KellerMedia.com and request a conversation, or call (800) 278-8706.

To take a free author, speaker or small business training webinar, go here: www.KellerMedia.com/Webinars

*On Facebook*: Follow us on Facebook: www.Facebook.com/KellerMediaInc

*On Twitter*: @KellerMediaInc

*On LinkedIn*: www.linkedin.com/in/KellerMedia

# Index